Kansas City Royals 2019

A Baseball Companion

Edited by Patrick Dubuque, Aaron Gleeman and Bret Sayre

Baseball Prospectus

Craig Brown and Dave Pease, Consultant Editors
Rob McQuown and Harry Pavlidis, Statistics Editors

Copyright © 2019 by DIY Baseball, LLC.
All rights reserved

This book or any part thereof may not be reproduced or transmitted in any form or by any means, electronic or mechanical, including photocopying, recording, or by any information storage and retrieval system, without permission in writing from the publisher.

Limit of Liability/Disclaimer of Warranty: While the publisher and the author have used their best efforts in preparing this book, they make no representations or warranties with respect to the accuracy or completeness of the contents of this book and specifically disclaim any implied warranties of merchantability or fitness for a particular purpose. No warranty may be created or extended by sales representatives or written sales materials. The advice and strategies contained herein may not be suitable for your situation. You should consult with a professional where appropriate. Neither the publisher nor the author shall be liable for any loss of profit or any other commercial damages, including but not limited to special, incidental, consequential, or other damages.

Library of Congress Cataloging-in-Publication Data:
paperback
ISBN-13: 978-1-949332-12-4

Project Credits
Cover Design: Kathleen Dyson
Interior Design and Production: Jeff Pease, Dave Pease
Layout: Jeff Pease, Dave Pease

Baseball icon courtesy of Uberux, from https://www.shareicon.net/author/uberux

Ballpark diagram courtesy of Lou Spirito/THIRTY81 Project, https://thirty81project.com/

Manufactured in the United States of America
10 9 8 7 6 5 4 3 2 1

Table of Contents

Foreword v
   Rob Mains

Statistical Introduction vii

Part 1: Team Analysis

Table for Two: Previewing the 2019 Kansas City Royals 3
   Craig Brown and Colby Wilson

Performance Graphs 7

2018 Team Performance 8

2019 Team Projections 9

Team Personnel 10

Kauffman Stadium Stats 11

Royals Team Analysis 13

Part 2: Player Analysis

Royals Player Analysis 20

Royals Prospects 103

Part 3: Featured Articles

The Hole in The Shift is Fixing Itself 117
   Russell Carleton

The State of the Quality Start 121
   Rob Mains

Heads-Up Hacking—The First Pitch 127
   Matthew Trueblood

A Hymn for the Index Stat 133
   Patrick Dubuque

Index of Names 137

Foreword

Rob Mains

Welcome to this companion of the 2019 Kansas City Royals. We at Baseball Prospectus are excited to provide this analysis of the Royals.

Our website, Baseball Prospectus, is a leader in delivering high-quality commentary and data to baseball fans everywhere. To some, those words—commentary and data—appear mutually exclusive. There are people out there who believe that traditional analysis and advanced analytics must run on different paths. But the simplistic narrative of stats vs. traditionalists just isn't true. Every team's analytics department interacts with scouting, development, and major league operations with a common goal: Delivering a championship. New technologies, like radar tracking of pitch speeds and movement, enable talent evaluators to focus on qualitative aspects of pitching like mechanics and pitch sequencing. In-game strategies like infield shifts, based on batters' hit tendencies, help turn balls in play into outs. Hitters use information to adjust their swings to maximize run production.

All these numbers can seem, at best, intimidating, and at worst, counterproductive to the casual fan. Even as technology and analysis have embedded themselves deeply into the way teams run, it can often feel like statistics create a displacement between the viewer and the sport, breaking them out of the action. And yet every fan incorporates the numbers to some degree; stats like batting average and earned run average, so fundamental to how we talk about performance, are actually complicated formulas. They don't bother people because those formulas have become second nature, as easy to translate as the action on the field.

Along the way, new statistics have entered baseball's lexicon. You'll see some of them, like on-base percentage (which measures a batter's ability to get on base via walk, hit batter, or hit), OPS (on-base plus slugging), and average exit velocity (the speed of balls off a hitter's bat) on broadcasts. Others, like DRC+, might well be new to you. Some of them have been well-defined to the public, others haven't. That lack of context has created ambiguity. Fans know that a ball hit 100 mph is scorched, but does that mean extra bases? (Not if it's hit on the ground or high in the air it doesn't.)

For those who are amenable to them, the new statistics can increase the enjoyment and understanding of the game. They can help fans identify when a pitcher is tiring, when a stolen base or a bunt attempt makes sense (and, more often, when it doesn't), or how a team's lineup might be constructed. Websites like Baseball Prospectus add to that understanding by weaving metrics into the narrative of the game. That's the goal of this publication: to take some of the newer, more complicated statistics and make them as intuitive as the ones on the back of old baseball cards.

But you don't need to love analytics to love baseball. The fans at BP who worked together to write this guide are captivated first and foremost by the game itself. We're drawn to Aaron Judge's power, Francisco Lindor's glove, Billy Hamilton's speed and Patrick Corbin's slider and don't need numbers to tell us why they're so mesmerizing. The underlying statistics provide depth to the game that we all love.

We hope you'll find that this guide helps you better understand the Royals. Our analysts have studied the team's major league personnel and its minor league affiliates to identify their strengths and weaknesses, both the obvious ones and those that only a careful dissection of players' performances—yes, including the data—can reveal. You don't need us to tell you who was good and who wasn't in 2018, but our models and writers can help you project how each player is going to perform this year and beyond, and appreciate the greatness of each new game as it unfolds. As in the sport itself, the human and analytic components combine to generate a deeper overall understanding.

Think back to the first time you saw a baseball game on a high-definition TV. You'd grown familiar with how the game looked and felt on a picture tube. But new TV allowed you to see details that you'd never seen before. That's how advanced statistics work. The game itself is why you're here and why you're buying this. (And, for that matter, why we wrote it.) The statistical measures provide the sharper focus, the detail, the depth of knowledge that you didn't have before, generating an overall superior picture. Enjoy the view.

—*Rob Mains is an author of Baseball Prospectus.*

Statistical Introduction

Sports are, fundamentally, a blend of athletic endeavor and storytelling. Baseball, like any other sport, tells its stories in so many ways: in the arc of a game from the stands or a season from the box scores, in photos, or even in numbers. At Baseball Prospectus, we understand that statistics don't replace observation or any of baseball's stories, but complement everything else that makes the game so much fun.

What stats help us with is with patterns and precision, variance and value. This book can help you learn things you may not see from watching a game or hundred, whether it's the path of a career over time or the breadth of the entire MLB. We'd also never ask you to choose between our numbers and the experience of viewing a game from the cheap seats or the comfort of your home; our publication combines running the numbers with observations and wisdom from some of the brightest minds we can find. But if you *do* want to learn more about the numbers beyond what's on the backs of player jerseys, let us help explain.

Offense

At the end of this past year, we've revised our methodology for determining batting value. Long-time readers of Baseball Prospectus will notice that we've retired True Average in favor of a new metric: Deserved Runs Created Plus (DRC+). Developed by Jonathan Judge and our stats team, this statistic measures everything a player does at the plate–reaching base, hitting for power, making outs, and moving runners over–and puts it on a scale where 100 equals league-average performance. A DRC+ of 150 is terrific, a DRC+ of 100 is average, and a DRC+ of 75 means you better be an excellent defender.

DRC+ also does a better job than any of our previous metrics in taking contextual factors into account. The model adjusts for how the park affects performance, but also for things like the talent of the opposing pitcher, value of different types of batted-ball events, league, temperature, and other factors. It's able to describe a player's expected offensive contribution than any other statistic we've found over the years, and also does a better job of predicting future performance as well.

The other aspect of run-scoring is baserunning, which we quantify using Baserunning Runs. BRR not only records the value of stolen bases (or getting caught in the act), but also accounts for a runner's ability to go first to third on a single or advance on a fly ball.

Defense

Where offensive value is *relatively* easy to identify and understand, defensive value is ... not. Over the past dozen years, the sabermetric community has focused mostly on stats based on zone data: a real-live human person records the type of batted ball and estimated landing location, and models are created that give expected outs. From there, you can compare fielders' actual outs to those expected ones. Simple, right?

Unfortunately, zone data has two major issues. First, zone data is recorded by commercial data providers who keep the raw data private unless you pay for it. (All the statistics we build in this book and on our website use public data as inputs.) That hurts our ability to test assumptions or duplicate results. Second, over the years it has become apparent that there's quite a bit of "noise" in zone-based fielding analysis. Sometimes the conclusions drawn from zone data don't hold up to scrutiny, and sometimes the different data provided by different providers don't look anything alike, giving wildly different results. Sometimes the hard-working professional stringers or scorers might unknowingly inflict unconscious bias into the mix: for example good fielders will often be credited with more expected outs despite the data, and ballparks with high press boxes tend to score more line drives than ones with a lower press box.

Enter our Fielding Runs Above Average (FRAA). For most positions, FRAA is built from play-by-play data, which allows us to avoid the subjectivity found in many other fielding metrics. The idea is this: count how many fielding plays are made by a given player and compare that to expected plays for an average fielder at their position (based on pitcher ground-ball tendencies and batter handedness). Then we adjust for park and base-out situations.

When it comes to catchers, our methodology is a little different thanks to the laundry list of responsibilities they're tasked with beyond just, well, catching and throwing the ball. By now you've probably heard about "framing" or the art of making umpires more likely to call balls outside the strike zone for strikes. To put this into one tidy number, we incorporate pitch tracking data (for the years it exists) and adjust for important factors like pitcher, umpire, batter, and home-field advantage using a mixed-model approach. This grants us a number for how many strikes the catcher is personally adding to (or subtracting from) his pitchers' performance ... which we then convert to runs added or lost using linear weights.

Framing is one of the biggest parts of determining catcher value, but we also take into account blocking balls from going past, whether a scorer deems it a passed ball or a wild pitch. We use a similar approach–one that really benefits from the pitch tracking data that tells us what ends up in the dirt and what doesn't. We also include a catcher's ability to prevent stolen bases and how well they field balls in play, and *finally* we come up with our FRAA for catchers.

Pitching

Both pitching and fielding make up the half of baseball that isn't run scoring: run prevention. Separating pitching from fielding is a tough task, and most recent pitching analysis has branched off from Voros McCracken's famous (and controversial) statement, "There is little if any difference among major-league pitchers in their ability to prevent hits on balls hit in the field of play." The research of the analytic community has validated this to some extent, and there are a host of "defense-independent" pitching measures that have been developed to try and extricate the effect of the defense behind a hurler from the pitcher's work.

Our solution to this quandary is Deserved Run Average (DRA), our core pitching metric. DRA looks like earned run average (ERA), the tried-and-true pitching stat you've seen on every baseball broadcast or box score from the past century, but it's very different. To start, DRA takes an event-by-event look at what the pitchers does, and adjusts the value of that event based on different environmental factors like park, batter, catcher, umpire, base-out situation, run differential, inning, defense, home field advantage, pitcher role, and temperature. That mixed model gives us a pitcher's expected contribution, similar to what we do for our DRC+ model for hitters and FRAA model for catchers. (Oh, and we also consider the pitcher's effect on basestealing and on balls getting past the catcher.)

It's important to note that DRA is set to the scale of runs allowed per nine innings (RA9) instead of ERA, which makes DRA's scale slightly higher than ERA's. The reason for this is because ERA tends to overrate three types of pitchers:

1. Pitchers who play in parks where scorers hand out more errors. Official scorers differ significantly in the frequency at which they assign errors to fielders.
2. Ground-ball pitchers, because a substantial proportion of errors occur on grounders.
3. Pitchers who aren't very good. Better pitchers often allow fewer unearned runs than bad pitchers, because good pitchers tend to find ways to get out of jams.

Since the last time you picked up an edition of this book, we've also made a few minor changes to DRA to make it better. Recent research into "tunneling"–the act of throwing consecutive pitches that appear similar from a batter's point of view until after the swing decision point–data has given us a new contextual factor to account for in DRA: plate distance. This refers to the distance between successive pitches as they approach the plate, and while it has a smaller effect than factors like velocity or whiff rate, it still can help explain pitcher strikeout rate in our model.

New Pitching Metrics for 2019

We're including a few "new" pitching metrics for 2019's suite of Baseball Prospectus publications, but you may be familiar with them if you've spent time scouring the internet for stats.

Fastball Percentage

Our fastball percentage (FB%) statistic measures how frequently a pitcher throws a pitch classified as a "fastball," measured as a percentage of overall pitches thrown. We qualify three types of fastballs:

1. The traditional four-seam fastball;
2. The two-seam fastball or sinker;
3. "Hard cutters," which are pitches that have the movement profile of a cut fastball and are used as the pitcher's primary offering or in place of a more traditional fastball.

For example, a pitcher with a FB% of 67 throws any combination of these three pitches about two-thirds of the time.

Whiff Rate

Everybody loves a swing and a miss, and whiff rate (WHF) measures how frequently pitchers induce a swinging strike. To calculate WHF, we add up all the pitches thrown that ended with a swinging strike, then divide that number by a pitcher's total pitches thrown. Most often, high whiff rates correlate with high strikeout rates (and overall effective pitcher performance).

Called Strike Probability

Called Strike Probability (CSP) is a number that represents the likelihood that all of a pitcher's pitches will be called a strike while controlling for location, pitcher and batter handedness, umpire and count. Here's how it works: on each pitch, our model determines how many times (out of 100) that a similar pitch was called for a strike given those factors mentioned above, and when normalized for each batter's strike zone. Then we average the CSP for all pitches thrown by a pitcher in a season, and that gives us the yearly CSP percentage you see in the stats boxes.

As you might imagine, pitchers with a higher CSP are more likely to work in the zone, where pitchers with a lower CSP are likely locating their pitches outside the normal strike zone, for better or for worse.

Projections

Many of you aren't turning to this book just for a look at what a player has done, but for a look at what a player is going to do: the PECOTA projections. PECOTA, initially developed by Nate Silver (who has moved on to greater fame as a political analyst), consists of three parts:

1. Major-league equivalencies, which use minor-league statistics to project how a player will perform in the major leagues;
2. Baseline forecasts, which use weighted averages and regression to the mean to estimate a player's current true talent level; and
3. Aging curves, which uses the career paths of comparable players to estimate how a player's statistics are likely to change over time.

With all those important things covered, let's take a look at what's in the book this year.

Team Prospectus

You bought this book to learn more about your favorite (or maybe least-favorite, who are we to judge?) team, so let's talk about them. After a thoughtful preview of the 2019 season, you'll be presented with our Team Prospectus. This outlines many of the key statistics for each team's 2018 season, as well as a very inviting stadium diagram.

First you'll find the Performance Graphs page. The first is the 2018 Hit List Ranking. This shows our Hit List Rank for the team on each day of the 2018 season and is intended to give you a picture of the ups and downs of the team's season, including their highest and lowest ranks of the year. Hit List Rank measures overall team performance and drives the Hit List Power Rankings at the baseballprospectus.com website.

The second graph is Committed Payroll and helps you see how the team's payroll has compared to the MLB and divisional average payrolls over time. Payroll figures are currents as of January 1, 2019; with so many free agents still unsigned as of this writing, the final 2018 figure will likely be significantly different for many teams. (In the meantime, you can always find the most current data at Baseball Prospectus' Cot's Baseball Contracts page.)

Kansas City Royals 2019

The third graph is Farm System Ranking and displays how the Baseball Prospectus prospect team has ranked the organization's farm system since 2007. It also indicates the highest and lowest ranks that the farm system achieved over that time.

We start the Team Performance page with the squad's unadjusted and third-order 2018 win-loss records, presented in divisional context. We then list the three highest performing hitters and pitchers by WARP for 2018. Beneath that are a host of other team statistics. **Pythag** presents an adjusted 2018 winning percentage, calculated by taking runs scored per game (**RS/G**) and runs allowed per game (**RA/G**) for the team, and running them through a version of Bill James' Pythagorean formula that was refined and improved by David Smyth and Brandon Heipp. (The formula is called "Pythagenpat," which is equally fun to type and to say.)

Next up is **DRC+**, described earlier, to indicate the overall hitting ability of the team either above or below league-average. Run prevention on the pitching side is covered by **DRA** (also mentioned earlier) and another metric: Fielding Independent Pitching (**FIP**), which calculates another ERA-like statistic based on strikeouts, walks, and home runs recorded. Defensive Efficiency Rating (**DER**) tells us the percentage of balls in play turned into outs for the team, and is a quick fielding shorthand that rounds out run prevention.

After that, we have several measures related to roster composition, as opposed to on-field performance. **B-Age** and **P-Age** tell us the average age of a team's batters and pitchers, respectively. **Salary** is the combined team payroll for all on-field players, and Doug Pappas' Marginal Dollars per Marginal Win (**M$/MW**) tells us how much money a team spent to earn production above replacement level.

Ending this batch of statistics is the number of disabled list days a team had over the season (**DL Days**) and the amount of salary paid to players on the disabled list (**$ on DL**); this final number is expressed as a percentage of total payroll.

Next to each of these stats, we've listed each team's MLB rank in that category from 1st to 30th. In this, 1st always indicates a positive outcome and 30th a negative outcome, except in the case of salary–1st is highest.

The Team Projections page is intended to convey the team's operational capacity entering the 2019 season. We start with the team's PECOTA projected record for 2019, again in divisional context. The **+/-** column indicates how many more or less wins the team is projected to get than they got in 2018. We then list the three highest projected hitters and pitchers by WARP for 2018. A brief farm system summary follows, with the team's top prospect and number of BP Top 101 Prospects. Finally, we list the key new players and departed players, along with their 2019 projected WARP.

Alex Bregman 3B

Born: 03/30/94 Age: 25 Bats: R Throws: R
Height: 6'0" Weight: 180 Origin: Round 1, 2015 Draft (#2 overall)

YEAR	TEAM	LVL	AGE	PA	R	2B	3B	HR	RBI	BB	K	SB	CS	AVG/OBP/SLG
2016	CCH	AA	22	285	54	16	2	14	46	42	26	5	3	.297/.415/.559
2016	FRE	AAA	22	83	17	6	0	6	15	5	12	2	1	.333/.373/.641
2016	HOU	MLB	22	217	31	13	3	8	34	15	52	2	0	.264/.313/.478
2017	HOU	MLB	23	626	88	39	5	19	71	55	97	17	5	.284/.352/.475
2018	HOU	MLB	24	705	105	51	1	31	103	96	85	10	4	.286/.394/.532
2019	HOU	MLB	25	675	96	38	3	23	78	73	107	12	4	.272/.359/.463

Breakout: 6%   Improve: 52%   Collapse: 5%   Attrition: 2%   MLB: 100%
Comparables: Anthony Rendon, David Wright, Pablo Sandoval

YEAR	TEAM	LVL	AGE	PA	DRC+	VORP	BABIP	BRR	FRAA	WARP
2016	CCH	AA	22	285	172	38.9	.286	1.6	SS(51): -3.4, 3B(11): 1.4	2.7
2016	FRE	AAA	22	83	161	10.0	.333	-1.2	SS(14): 2.1, LF(3): -0.1	0.8
2016	HOU	MLB	22	217	107	9.6	.317	0.5	3B(40): 0.9, SS(6): -0.1	1.1
2017	HOU	MLB	23	626	114	34.7	.311	-1.5	3B(132): 8.7, SS(30): -2.9	3.9
2018	HOU	MLB	24	705	150	72.6	.289	-1.6	3B(136): 5.4, SS(28): -0.4	7.4
2019	HOU	MLB	25	675	125	37.3	.295	0.0	3B 7, SS 0	4.6

After the projections page, we share a few items about the team's home ballpark. There's the aforementioned diagram of the park's dimensions (including distances to the outfield wall), a few important biographical facts about the stadium, a graphic showing the height of the wall from the left-field pole to the right-field pole, and a table showing three-year park factors for the stadium. The park factors are displayed as indexes where 100 is average, 110 means that the park inflates the statistic in question by 10 percent, and 90 means that the park deflates the statistic in question by 10 percent.

Following the ballpark page, we have a **Personnel** section that lists many of the important decision-makers and upper-level field and operations staff members for the franchise, as well as any former Baseball Prospectus staff members who are currently part of the organization.

Position Players

After all that information and a thoughtful bylined essay covering each team, we present our player comments. Each player is listed with the major-league team who employed him as of early January 2019. If a player changed teams after that point via free agency, trade, or any other method, you'll be able to find them in the book for their previous squad.

First, we cover biographical information (age is as of June 30, 2019) before moving onto the stats themselves. Our statistic columns include standard identifying information like **YEAR**, **TEAM**, **LVL** (level of affiliated play) and **AGE** before getting into the numbers. Next, we provide raw, unstranslated numbers like you might find on the back of your dad's baseball cards: **PA** (plate appearances), **R** (runs), **2B** (doubles), **3B** (triples), **HR** (home runs), **RBI** (runs batted in), **BB** (walks), **K** (strikeouts), **SB** (stolen bases) and **CS** (caught stealing). Then we have unadjusted "slash" statistics: **AVG** (batting average), **OBP** (on-base percentage) and **SLG** (slugging percentage).

Just below the stats box is **PECOTA** data, which is discussed further in a following section. After that, it's on to a pithy and always-informative comment written by a member of the Baseball Prospectus staff, before we cover more stats.

The second text box repeats YEAR, TEAM, LVL, AGE, and PA, then moves on to **DRC+** (Deserved Runs Created Plus), which we described earlier as total offensive expected contribution compared to the league average. Next, one of our oldest active metrics, **VORP** (Value Over Replacement Player), considers offensive production, position and plate appearances. In essence, it is the number of runs contributed beyond what a replacement-level player at the same position would contribute if given the same percentage of team plate appearances. VORP does not consider the quality of a player's defense.

BABIP (batting average on balls in play) tells us how often a ball in play fell for a hit, and can help us identify whether a batter may have been lucky or not … but note that high BABIPs also tend to follow the great hitters of our time, as well as speedy singles hitters who put the ball on the ground.

The next item is **BRR** (Baserunning Runs), which covers all of a player's baserunning accomplishments which includes (but isn't limited to) swiped bags and failed attempts. Next is **FRAA** (Fielding Runs Above Average), which also includes the number of games previously played at each position noted in parentheses. Multi-position players have only their two most frequent positions listed here, but their total FRAA number reflects all positions played.

Our last column here is **WARP** (Wins Above Replacement Player). WARP estimates the total value of a player, which means for hitters it takes into account hitting runs above average (calculated using the DRC+ model), BRR and FRAA. Then, it makes an adjustment for positions played and gives the player a credit for plate appearances based upon the difference between "replacement level"¬–which is derived from the quality of players added to a team's roster after the start of the season¬–and the league average.

Catchers

Catchers are a special breed, and thus they have earned their own separate box which displays some of the defensive metrics that we've built just for them. As an example, let's check out J.T. Realmuto.

YEAR	TEAM	P. COUNT	FRM RUNS	BLK RUNS	THRW RUNS	TOT RUNS
2016	MIA	18935	-8.5	1.8	2.1	-5.6
2017	MIA	18959	5.3	1.7	1.0	9.1
2018	MIA	16399	-0.4	0.9	0.1	0.4
2019	PHI	18448	-1.4	1.5	0.7	0.8

The **YEAR** and **TEAM** columns match what you'd find in the other stat box. **P. COUNT** indicates the number of pitches thrown while the catcher was behind the plate, including swinging strikes, fouls, and balls in play. **FRM RUNS** is the total run value the catcher provided (or cost) his team by influencing the umpire to call strikes where other catchers did not. **BLK RUNS** expresses the total run value above or below average for the catcher's ability to prevent wild pitches and passed balls. **THRW RUNS** is calculated using a similar model as the previous two statistics, and it measures a catcher's ability to throw out basestealers but also to dissuade them from testing his arm in the first place. It takes into account factors like the pitcher (including his delivery and pickoff move) and baserunner (who could be as fast as Billy Hamilton or as slow as Yonder Alonso). **TOT RUNS** is the sum of all of the previous three statistics.

Pitchers

Let's give our pitchers a turn, using 2018 NL Cy Young winner Jacob deGrom as our example. Take a look at his first stat block: the first line and the **YEAR**, **TEAM**, **LVL** and **AGE** columns are the same as in the position player example earlier.

Here too, we have a series of columns that display raw, unadjusted statistics compiled by the pitcher over the course of a season: **W** (wins), **L** (losses), **SV** (saves), **G** (games pitched), **GS** (games started), **IP** (innings pitched), **H** (hits allowed) and **HR** (home runs allowed). Next we have two statistics that are rates: **BB/9** (walks per nine innings) and **K/9** (strikeouts per nine innings), before returning to the unadjusted **K** (strikeouts).

Next up is **GB%** (ground ball percentage), which is the percentage of all batted balls that were hit in the ground, including both outs and hits. Remember, this is based on observational data and subject to human error, so please approach this with a healthy dose of skepticism.

BABIP (batting average on balls in play) is calculated using the same methodology as it is for position players, but it often tells us more about a pitcher than it does a hitter. With pitchers, a high BABIP is often due to poor defense or bad luck, and can often be an indicator of potential rebound, and a low BABIP may be cause to expect performance regression. (A typical league-average BABIP is close to .290-.300.)

After a witty 150ish words on the player like only Baseball Prospectus's staff can provide, it's on to that second stat block, which repeats the YEAR, TEAM, LVL, and AGE columns. The metrics **WHIP** (walks plus hits per inning pitched) and **ERA**

Kansas City Royals 2019

(earned run average) are old standbys: WHIP measures walks and hits allowed on a per-inning basis, while ERA measures earned runs on a nine-inning basis. Neither of these stats are translated or adjusted.

DRA (Deserved Run Average) was described at length earlier, and measures how many runs the pitcher "deserved" to allow per nine innings. Please note that since we lack all the data points that would make for a "real" DRA for minor-league events, the DRA displayed for minor league partial-seasons is based off of different data. (That data is a modified version of our cFIP metric, which you can find more information about on our website.)

Jacob deGrom RHP
Born: 06/19/88   Age: 31   Bats: L   Throws: R
Height: 6'4"   Weight: 180   Origin: Round 9, 2010 Draft (#272 overall)

YEAR	TEAM	LVL	AGE	W	L	SV	G	GS	IP	H	HR	BB/9	K/9	K	GB%	BABIP
2016	NYN	MLB	28	7	8	0	24	24	148	142	15	2.2	8.7	143	47%	.312
2017	NYN	MLB	29	15	10	0	31	31	201¹	180	28	2.6	10.7	239	48%	.305
2018	NYN	MLB	30	10	9	0	32	32	217	152	10	1.9	11.2	269	48%	.281
2019	NYN	MLB	31	13	9	0	31	31	186	145	18	2.3	10.7	221	46%	.286

Breakout: 8%   Improve: 29%   Collapse: 28%   Attrition: 6%   MLB: 85%
Comparables: Erik Bedard, A.J. Burnett, CC Sabathia

YEAR	TEAM	LVL	AGE	WHIP	ERA	DRA	WARP	MPH	FB%	WHF	CSP
2016	NYN	MLB	28	1.20	3.04	3.30	3.5	96.3	59.6	12.1	47.2
2017	NYN	MLB	29	1.19	3.53	3.02	5.7	97.2	55.5	14.5	49.5
2018	NYN	MLB	30	0.91	1.70	2.09	8.0	98.2	52.1	16.3	48.4
2019	NYN	MLB	31	1.02	2.91	3.23	3.9	96.6	54.5	14.8	48.2

Just like with hitters, **WARP** (Wins Above Replacement Player) is a total value metric that puts pitchers of all stripes on the same scale as position players. We use DRA as the primary input for our calculation of WARP. You might notice that relief pitchers (due to their limited innings) may have a lower WARP than you were expecting or than you might see in other WARP-like metrics. WARP does not take leverage into account, just the actions a pitcher performs and the expected value of those actions ... which ends up judging high-leverage relief pitchers differently than you might imagine given their prestige and market value.

MPH gives you the pitcher's 95th percentile velocity for the noted season, in order to give you an idea of what the *peak* fastball velocity a pitcher possesses. Since this comes from our pitch tracking data, it is not publicly available for minor-league pitchers.

Finally, we display the three new pitching metrics we described earlier. **FB%** (fastball percentage) gives you the percentage of fastballs thrown out of all pitches. **WhiffRt** (whiff rate) tells you the percentage of swinging strikes induced out of all pitches. **CS Prob** (called strike probability) expresses the likelihood of all pitches thrown to result in a called strike, after controlling for factors like handedness, umpire, pitch type, count, and location.

PECOTA

All players have PECOTA projections for 2019, as well as a set of other numbers that describe the performance of comparable players according to PECOTA. All projections for 2019 are for the player at the date we went to press in early January and are projected into the league and park context as indicated by the team abbreviation. All PECOTA projected statistics represent a player's projected major-league performance.

The numbers beneath the player's stats–Breakout, Improve, Collapse, Attrition–are part and parcel of the PECOTA projections. They estimate the likelihood of changes in performance relative to the player's previously-established level of production, based on the performance of comparable players:

Breakout Rate is the percent change that a player's production will improve by at least 20 percent relative to the weighted average of his performance over his most recent seasons.

Improve Rate is the percent chance that a player's production will improve at all relative to his baseline performance. A player who is expected to perform just the same as he has in the recent past will have an Improve Rate of 50 percent.

Collapse Rate is the percent chance that a position player's production will decline by at least 25 percent relative to his baseline performance.

Attrition Rate operates on playing time rather than performance. Specifically, it measures the likelihood that a player's playing time will decrease by at least 50 percent relative to his established level.

Breakout Rate and Collapse Rate can sometimes be counterintuitive for players who have already experienced a radical change in performance level. It's also worth noting that the projected decline in a player's rate performances might not be indicative of an expected decline in underlying ability or skill, but could just be an anticipated correction following a breakout season.

MLB% is the percentage of similar players who played in the major leagues in their relevant season.

The final pieces of information are the player's three highest-scoring comparable players as determined by PECOTA. All comparables represent a snapshot of how the listed player was performing at the same age as the current player, so if a 23-year-old pitcher is compared to Bartolo Colon, he's actually being compared to a 23-year-old Colon, not the version that pitched for the Rangers in 2018, nor to Colon's career as a whole.

A few points about pitcher projections. First, we aren't yet projecting peak velocity, so that column will be blank in the PECOTA lines. Second, projecting DRA is trickier than evaluating past performance, because it is unclear how deserving each pitcher will be of his anticipated outcomes. However, we know that another DRA-related statistic–contextual FIP or cFIP–estimates future run scoring very well. So for PECOTA, the projected DRA figures you see are based on the past cFIPs generated by the pitcher and comparable players over time, along with the other factors described above.

Lineouts

In each chapter's Lineouts section, you'll find abbreviated text comments, as well as most of same information you'd find in our full player comments. We limit the stats boxes in this section to only including the 2018 information for each player.

Exclusive Player Visualizations

In our constant battle to provide you with new and interesting baseball content you can't find anywhere else, we've added a trio of data visualizations to each hitter's entry in these books and a pair of visualizations for each pitcher.

For hitters, you'll find three new infographics. The first is each player's **Batted Ball Distribution**, which displays the five major sections of the field: LF (left), LCF (left center), CF (center), RCF (right center), and RF (right). The percentage indicated tells us what percentage of batted balls from that hitter fell within that part of the field during the 2018 season. We've also included the hitter's slugging percentage on balls in play (also called **SLGCON**) for that part of the field.

You'll also see two heatmaps: **Strike Zone vs LHP** and **Strike Zone vs RHP**. These heat maps represent a view of the strike zone from behind the catcher. Areas where there is a darker coloration represent the places where a higher percentage of pitches resulted in hits. In other words, the heatmap represents a hitter's "sweet spots" for getting hits against either left-handed or right-handed pitchers, depending on the image.

Pitchers get two images that help explain what their pitches look like from a hitter's perspective: **Pitch Shape vs LHH** and **Pitch Shape vs RHH**. These images show you the shape and the "tunneling" effect of each pitcher's offerings from the batter's perspective. For each type of pitch that a pitcher throws (represented by an indicator shape), there's a set of dots indicating the flight path, where each dot represents a 0.01-second interval. This maps the average trajectory and speed of an offering, ending where the ball crosses the plate. The solid black box represents the regular strike zone, while the gray contour lines indicate the range of locations that a pitcher typically works in.

Below the image, we provide a bit more detailed information about each pitcher's average offering in the **Pitch Types** box. Here, we also list each of the pitcher's major offerings under the **Type** column.

- **Fastballs** (which usually refers to the four-seam variation)
- **Sinkers** and/or two-seam fastballs
- **Cutters** (which could include "hard" cutters like cut fastballs and "soft" cutters that resemble hard sliders)
- **Changeups** (not including most splitters)
- **Splitters** (split-fingered pitches, forkballs, and some split-changes)
- **Sliders** and/or slurves
- **Curveballs** (including spike-curveballs and knuckle-curveballs, as well as some slurvy curves)
- **Slow curveballs** and/or eephus pitches
- **Knuckleballs**
- **Screwballs**

The **Freq** column indicates the percentage of overall pitches that fall into each of those type categories; if a pitcher has a 16.55% score for changeups, then that's the percent of all pitches that he throws as changeups. **Velo** is exactly what you think it is: the average miles per hour for each pitch type. **H Mov** is the number of inches of horizontal movement on the average pitch of that type, while **V Mov** is the number of inches of vertical movement on the average pitch of that type. (At Baseball Prospectus, we measure this over the long flight of the ball and include gravity into the V Mov number in order to give you the most realistic representation of what the pitch *actually* does.)

If you're wondering about the second number in brackets, that's the index for that velocity or movement compared to the league average. Like DRC+, a score of 100 means that the speed or movement is about the same as league average, while a higher score means that there's higher velocity or movement than the league average. Numbers below 100 indicate less velocity or movement than the league average.

Part 1: Team Analysis

Table for Two: Previewing the 2019 Kansas City Royals

Craig Brown and Colby Wilson

CRAIG BROWN: Here's a team four years removed from a World Championship and one year removed from 104 losses. There's a lot of work to be done before the Royals can get back into contention. If we're to follow the lead of Dayton Moore, we are forbidden from using the "R" word when discussing the Royals' current situation. But—big question—these Royals should be improved from last year, right?

COLBY WILSON: Good question. I don't know about improved–they recently signed Jake Diekman, a serviceable arm who now projects as the Royals second-best reliever by DRA. So I'll stop short of improved, but I will say more interesting. I think so much of the frustration last season was less with the losing than with the perfunctory fashion in which it came. They'll be a more entertaining sort of bad; I'll take that. What say you?

CRAIG: Last year's team was bad and boring. I'll take not as bad and somewhat entertaining. They're certainly going to run. Two-time AL steals leader Whit Merrifield will be paired with Adalberto Mondesi at the top of the order. You figure newcomer Billy Hamilton will slot into the ninth spot in the lineup. Then, it's stolen base city. PECOTA projects 43 steals for Mondesi, 37 for Hamilton and 33 for Merrifield. That's 113 steals. That would have ranked them seventh in the league last year… Behind the Kansas City Royals. And that's not even acknowledging professional pinch runner Terrance Gore, who is projected for 20 steals. Speed thrills, baby. This is the identity for the 2019 Royals, isn't it?

COLBY: Gotta be, and it's the most exciting part of this little journey we're going to embark on here. I've been beating this drum for a while now, but the smart move is to run and run and never stop running; they've cornered the market on speed. The logical extension is to make those PECOTA projections look hilariously low by season's end.

If you ask me (and I suppose that is what we're doing here), Gore is the avatar for the 2019 Kansas City Royals: He's fast, he's cheap and he's probably going to be playing somewhere else by the end of July. All these fliers the Royals are taking… if even half pan out, the prospect haul near the trade deadline could be significant and it's low-key the thing I haven't heard many people discussing so far. By the end of July, the Royals will probably be worse as a club but better as a franchise, if that makes sense.

CRAIG: That makes sense and that's exactly what a club in the Royals current situation (still avoiding the "R" word here) should be doing. While this team was vastly improved last September compared to the previous five months, that's not exactly a jumping off point. They are hitting the reset button come Opening Day 2019, still looking toward a future.

Speaking of last September, the club seemed to get a bit of a spark from the promotions and everyday playing time of the aforementioned Mondesi and Ryan O'Hearn. O'Hearn is an interesting player to consider. He clubbed 12 bombs in 179 plate appearances and finished with a 130 DRC+. An amazing start to a career. PECOTA isn't buying it, though, projecting him for a full season of 20 home runs while hitting .219/.299/.405 with a DRC+ of 86. That's… it? Really? Is O'Hearn the Royals' latest paper tiger?

COLBY: Royals people have seemed divided over O'Hearn for ages, and PECOTA's projections outline the best and worst of those arguments. He's got power! He's got holes in his swing you could drive an F-350 through! I'm bearish; I see him as a placeholder for Nick Pratto at best and a KBO All-Star at worst. Of course, I said that when he got called up last year and he put up Fred McGriff numbers for two months. Maybe I'm not very good at this.

More fascinating to me (and you, because I know you've had thoughts on this forever) is Jorge Soler. PECOTA has him being healthy for the first time during his Royals career; productive is another matter entirely. He hasn't been The Masher Who Was Promised after coming over for Wade Davis; is this the final referendum on Jorge Soler?

CRAIG: Ahhh… Has there been another player as nondescript in this post World Series era for the Royals as Soler? It's OK if you haven't thought of him; he hasn't been on the field all that much and when he has the results have just been meh. PECOTA sees what amounts to a continuation for him with a DRC+ of 101. That's certainly not what the Royals thought they were getting when they dealt for him, but I suppose if he can stay out of the trainer's room and post league-average offensive numbers they would probably take that at this point.

Mentioning Soler brings up this alleged logjam the Royals have in the outfield. You have Hamilton penciled in as the everyday center fielder. Assume Alex Gordon in the final year of his contract is the incumbent in left. That leaves right field and DH to be split among the group of Soler, Brian Goodwin, Jorge Bonifacio and Brett Phillips. None of these four exactly sets PECOTA's circuits aflutter. Phillips is the guy who has intrigued me since arriving in the Mike Moustakas trade with Milwaukee last summer. He has the arm to play right and has that former top prospect luster. Is he *the* guy, or is he just a guy?

COLBY: I still don't get anyone's fascination with Goodwin in regards to this particular team. He's fine. Fine! Totally fine. If you're a contender in need of a fourth outfielder/late game speed/pinch-hitter near the end of the bench, you'll do a lot worse than Brian Goodwin. But the Royals are not a contender, and so having Goodwin around to be jusssssst good enough to steal at-bats from the Jorge's and Phillips has never made sense to me. You could make this same argument about Gore, but he's not taking at-bats from anybody.

Phillips has everything at extremes; he's extremely talented defensively, extremely fast, extremely limited offensively and extremely goofy, which is a personality trait that (fair or not) has not always found a welcome home with Dayton Moore's Royals. I like Phillips a lot; with some patience and continued reps, he's got a chance to be a contributor the next time this franchise is decent. I don't know that he'll get it, and that disappoints me because he's fun to watch and super talented and I think those should outweigh whatever flakiness points he loses for his personality–which, again, is something fun that baseball should try to have more of.

CRAIG: We haven't really talked about the pitching up to this point. Which is probably for the best, given how dreadful it was last season. They haven't done anything to address the rotation and are clearly counting on Danny Duffy, Brad Keller and Jakob Junis to be their front three. Keller in particular is interesting to me. He finished with a 3.08 ERA and 4.87 DRA. He doesn't miss many bats—his nine percent whiff rate was about two points below the league average—and seems a candidate to regress.

COLBY: My stock answer to anyone who asks to talk about the Royals pitching is, "Oh, could we not?" But if you insist.

Naturally, Keller would be a prime candidate for regression; 12 months ago, he was a Rule 5 pick by the pitching-starved Reds and immediately dealt to the Royals. If the Reds don't want you, sometimes that's really bad news for a pitcher (see Bailey, Homer). As you alluded to, DRA doesn't think much of him; his 4.87 DRA was nearly two runs higher than his 3.08 ERA, which... that's the kind of difference reserved for the David Hess', Tyler Chatwood's and Hector Santiago's of the world. That whiff rate? That's Homer Bailey territory, baby. Jhoulys Chacin territory. Tanner Roark territory.

That said, the slider and change both rated out as plus-pitches for him a year ago. They induce weak contact and make up for a fastball that is fine but by no means a world-beater. The league has a season's worth of information on him now. Not to turd up this punch bowl, but expecting a repeat performance from his rookie campaign may not be the way to go.

CRAIG: When you put it that way... So let's jump in the time machine and leap ahead seven months from now. Where do the Royals end up? How do they get there?

Kansas City Royals 2019

COLBY: Well, I'd love to say they'll be better than they were last year. And they should be! From a purely talent-based view, no part of the roster is worse right now than it was for most of last season. Even the impending move of your fav Ian Kennedy to the bullpen is theoretically sound.

But a great many of the assets added were added with the idea of flipping them later. I'm excited about all the speed but I may not feel the same way when Hamilton and Gore are in different unis and half the bullpen has been shipped to a contender (hopefully!); as we saw with the Jon Jay move last year, Dayton Moore is not afraid to deal when an asset is at its most valuable. Honestly… the most memorable part of this season may happen on Draft Night. Come on Bobby Witt Jr.!

CRAIG: Ohhh… Draft Night should definitely be a party. I too think they should be better than last year, although former Royals manager Buddy Bell once warned that you never say you've hit rock bottom because it could always get worse. He was a fun guy during the close of the Allard Baird era, wasn't he? PECOTA has Kansas City at 72 wins and while the computers and spreadsheets have always hated the Royals, this seems about right.

As you mentioned, Moore knows the focus is on the farm system, so anyone on a one year deal is trade fodder. Hamilton, Boxburger, Deikman and guys on minor league contracts like Homer Bailey and Drew Storen—if they stick—are all candidates to be shipped off to a contender. There's not a lot in the upper minors to help, but Richard Lovelady and Nicky Lopez seem like they're ready for their audition. The pipeline is slow at the moment, but it is moving.

It smells like a fourth place finish in the AL Central.

COLBY: Yikes. So we don't close this out on that low of a note, I feel like we should acknowledge that none of the rest of this division is any great shakes, either. The White Sox pursuit of Manny Machado has largely yielded extended family members and assorted friends who aren't Machado and the Tigers are even more of a trash fire than the Royals; the Tribe will probably still win this in a walk, but there's no reason the Royals can't challenge for a third place or even a (VERY distant) second place finish in a division where the Twins can fire the manager, lose the franchise's most distinct player since Kirby Puckett, see its two top prospects wander through miserable seasons… and not only be tabbed to finish second in the division, but be the obvious choice. I would never say you should expect great things from the 2019 Royals, but somebody has to win games in the AL Central and it might as well be them.

CRAIG: Damn the "R" word! Let's replace it with the more optimistic "M" word. Mediocre.

COLBY: I like it, which is not something one should ever say regarding the word 'Mediocre.'

Performance Graphs

2018 Hit List Ranking

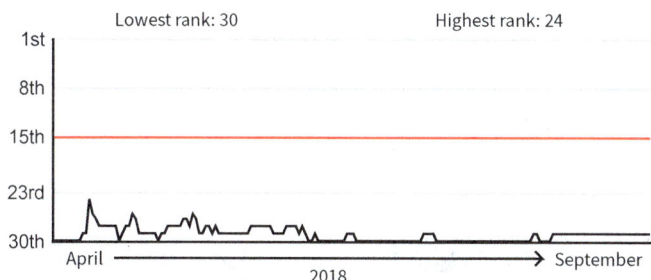

Committed Payroll (in millions)

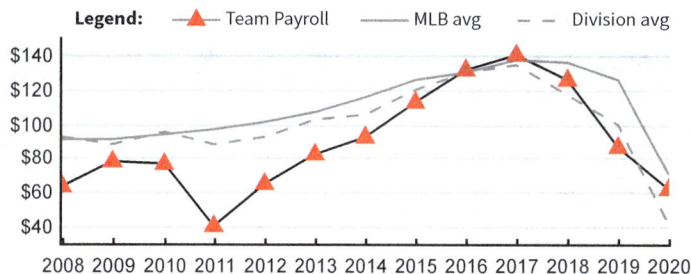

Farm System Ranking

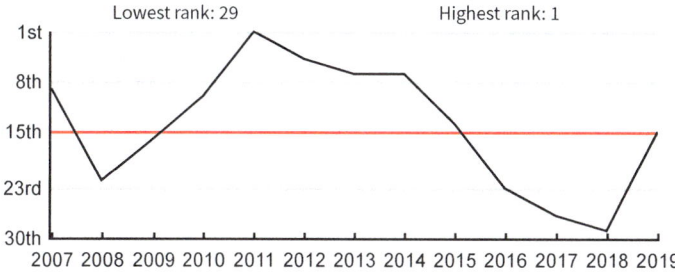

2018 Team Performance

ACTUAL STANDINGS

Team	W	L	Pct
CLE	91	71	.561
MIN	78	84	.481
DET	64	98	.395
CHA	62	100	.382
KCA	**58**	**104**	**.358**

THIRD-ORDER STANDINGS

Team	W	L	Pct
CLE	92	70	.567
MIN	70	92	.432
DET	62	100	.382
CHA	61	101	.376
KCA	**58**	**104**	**.358**

TOP HITTERS

Player	WARP
Whit Merrifield	4.4
Adalberto Mondesi	1.6
Salvador Perez	1.3

TOP PITCHERS

Player	WARP
Scott Barlow	0.9
Brad Keller	0.6
Kevin McCarthy	0.4

VITAL STATISTICS

Statistic Name	Value	Rank
Pythagenpat	.377	28th
Runs Scored per Game	3.94	25th
Runs Allowed per Game	5.14	26th
Deserved Runs Created Plus	92	21st
Deserved Run Average	5.62	28th
Fielding Independent Pitching	4.69	27th
Defensive Efficiency Rating	.691	29th
Batter Age	28.6	22nd
Pitcher Age	27.6	11th
Salary	$124.7M	20th
Marginal $ per Marginal Win	$11.8M	2nd
Disabled List Days	$1,302.0M	22nd
$ on DL	13%	9th

2019 Team Projections

PROJECTED STANDINGS

Team	W	L	Pct	+/-
CLE	97	65	.598	+6
MIN	82	80	.506	+4
KCA	**72**	**90**	**.444**	**+14**
CHA	70	92	.432	+8
DET	67	95	.413	+3

TOP PROJECTED HITTERS

Player	WARP
Martin Maldonado	4
Whit Merrifield	3.2
Adalberto Mondesi	2.4

TOP PROJECTED PITCHERS

Player	WARP
Jake Junis	1.8
Brad Keller	1.5
Danny Duffy	1.3

FARM SYSTEM REPORT

Top Prospect	Number of Top 101 Prospects
Seuly Matias, #52	3

KEY DEDUCTIONS

Player	WARP

KEY ADDITIONS

Player	WARP
Martin Maldonado	4
Billy Hamilton	0.9
Chris Owings	0.6
Brad Boxberger	0.5
Jake Diekman	0.4

Team Personnel

General Manager
Dayton Moore

AGM, Player Personnel
J.J. Picollo

AGM, MLB & International Ops
Rene Francisco

Assistant General Manager
Scott Sharp

Manager
Ned Yost

BP Alumni
Daniel Mack

Kauffman Stadium Stats

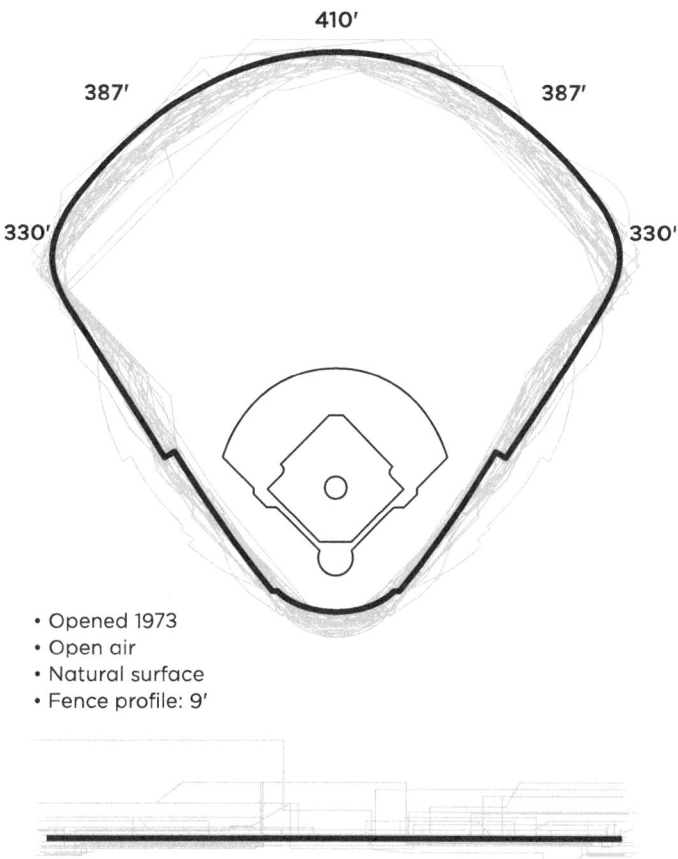

- Opened 1973
- Open air
- Natural surface
- Fence profile: 9'

Three-Year Park Factors

Runs	Runs/RH	Runs/LH	HR/RH	HR/LH
101	102	98	93	89

Royals Team Analysis

It's a good thing flags fly forever. The Royals' 2015 pennant feels like a lifetime ago.

Time is unforgiving, especially in baseball. Win a championship? That was great. Now, do it again. Yesterday was so much fun and we'll never forget the good times, but what are you going to do for me today? The fiscal realities of the game mean it's difficult to keep together a title-winning team for an extended period. That can go for double in baseball's smaller markets. This is nothing new. It's the economics of certainty.

After winning back-to-back American League pennants and reaching the summit in 2015, the goal in Kansas City was to keep their window of contention open as long as possible. Knowing their core players were under team control through at least the 2017 season, the Royals went for the ring again in 2016, spending $72 million to retain Alex Gordon and another $70 million and a first-round draft pick to add Ian Kennedy. For good measure, they splashed the cash on their bullpen, bringing back Joakim Soria on a $25 million deal. Payroll jumped to $131 million, rarefied air for a team of the Royals' means, and placing them firmly in baseball's middle class.

They won 81 games and finished in third place.

Undaunted, they went for it one final time the following season. They didn't make the same kind of noisy free agent signings, but the Royals did refuse to trade their most valuable assets in impending free agents Eric Hosmer, Mike Moustakas and Lorenzo Cain. Payroll increased to $143 million, which again placed the Royals in the middle of the fiscal pack.

They won 80 games and finished in third place.

And just like that, the Royals' window of contention slammed shut.

⚾ ⚾ ⚾

That quick rehash of the recent past wasn't meant as a direct history lesson, per se. Rather, it's a look into how the Royals' front office operates under general manager Dayton Moore, which is important when attempting to understand what comes next. Moore and his staff knew the reckoning was rapidly arriving, yet they still sought to delay the grim necessity of a rebuild as long as possible.

They would spend money. They would trade prospects. They would attempt to compete. Damn the realities. They felt they owed at least that much to their players and their fans.

Sometimes, you can trip over sentimentality. Your head tells you to do one thing, while your heart pulls you in another direction. In this instance, neglecting the realities of the situation by chasing that elusive spot in the postseason, the Royals simply delayed the inevitable. They neglected the future because they were so focused on the present. By refusing to trade their most valuable players in exchange for cost-controlled prospects to stock the organization, they dug a deeper hole for themselves once the rebuild commenced. As Stinger once told Maverick, the Royals' ego was writing checks their body couldn't cash.

Most teams in the Royals' position would go for a full teardown. The middle ground—that area the Royals occupied in 2016 and 2017—is now considered the equivalent of baseball's Siberia. In this no-man's land, the abyss occupied between 75 and 89 wins is where a franchise isn't good enough to qualify for the postseason and not bad enough to restock the farm system with top-10 picks. Lather, rinse, repeat. It turns out there's a high price to pay for mediocrity.

⚾ ⚾ ⚾

Here's where things get tricky. Yes, it's obvious at this point that the Royals should tear everything down, absorb the losses on the field in the short term and begin constructing a plan to rebuild for the long term. Yet forget about losing today to build for tomorrow. Moore abhors the idea of losing, any time. That shapes his philosophy as a general manager more than just about anything else. They will not tank and they are loathe to use the term rebuild when describing where they are in their process. They pursued bringing back Hosmer. They took advantage of a stagnant free agent market and re-signed Moustakas. They were happy to stake out that middle ground. To Moore, tanking is cheating the paying customer and rebuilding is a three-syllable word for making excuses.

That's fine and all, but it ignored the harsh reality that the 2018 Royals just weren't going to be any good. They entered the season knowing wins would be difficult to come by, but they didn't expect the utter wretchedness that would define their team through the first five months. Internal expectations pegged them closer to 72 wins. Maybe 67 if they couldn't catch a few breaks. But 58? Somehow, they found that number to be unimaginable. It was the reality. They still insisted they were not among the teams tanking and losing on purpose, but how could you tell?

From June 1 to the All-Star break, they won seven times in 39 games. In August, they dropped to 52 games below .500, the furthest behind the break-even point in franchise history. They were, at one point, on pace to lose almost 115 games.

They were giving the Baltimore Orioles a race to the bottom of the pile and the right to select first in the 2019 draft. They were boring and they were dreadful. It was, frankly, a chore to watch them play.

If they weren't tanking, then what the hell were they doing?

⚾ ⚾ ⚾

During the first go-around (known, now fondly, in Kansas City as simply, The Process) it took Moore and his staff close to five years to build a minor-league system that would be the envy of baseball. The Farm System Ranking in the sidebar shows the organization at no. 1 in 2011, but that doesn't quite do the overall strength of the system at that time proper justice. In that year's publication, Royals minor leaguers occupied 10 spots in BP's Top 101 Prospects list. By the time the Royals slammed into the end of their competitive window, the prospect cupboard was bare. (Again, refer to the Farm System Ranking that resembles a stockbroker's nightmare or an Austrian downhill course Lindsay Von would attack.)

Trades, player development busts and a few years of questionable drafting with later-round picks due to their major-league success conspired to strip a once-envied system into one most notable for an abyss of impact talent. So the Royals set about assembling depth. The ascent from close to rock bottom has begun. It's not a sexy farm system, but it's functional. The bad drafts and the trades made during the championship years mean there's little of potential impact in the upper levels, and it's likely to remain that way for another year or two. Indeed, the marrow of the minors was found last summer with the Single-A Lexington Legends. Six of the organization's current top 10 prospects spent some or all of 2018 playing for the Sally League champs.

The Royals will take most of that group and bump them a level this season. And they'll repeat the process for the next year, and then probably the next, keeping the majority together until they're ready to break into the majors. This is The Process 2.0. The blueprint of this rebuild can be found in the roots of the original Process when Hosmer, Moustakas, Danny Duffy and others joined forces at the lower levels of the organization and started charging to minor-league championships before arriving in Kansas City. It's about creating a culture of winning that's important to Moore. You undercut that culture when you lose on purpose to position yourself for future success. Moore has done it before. He has a ring. He trusts his process. But this time may be different.

The Process 2.0 is unique in that it abhors the losses generally marked by rebuilding. While restocking the minors is happening, the major-league team is looking for major-league players. Or in Royals parlance, action-type players. They spent $3 million on Chris Owings to be a utilityman. They tossed $5.25 million at Billy Hamilton. They gave Terrance Gore—owner of one hit and 27 steals spread over five big-league seasons—a major-league contract. These are the offseason moves of a marginal contender looking to fill a few areas of need with moderately useful players. On the Royals, they will be counted on to save the team from 95 losses. They are not tanking.

The Process 2.0 cares not for conventional wisdom.

⚾   ⚾   ⚾

It's still a rebuild, damnit, even if the Royals don't want to use that word. For The Process 2.0 to work they'll need pitching, and the Royals know better than perhaps any other team how difficult it is to develop starting pitching.

Thanks to last offseason's free agents signing elsewhere after rejecting qualifying offers, the Royals entered the 2018 draft with the highest signing bonus pool available. They leveraged every dollar, going over-slot with their first-round selection, Florida Gators right-hander Brady Singer, and following that pick with four more college arms in the first two rounds. They broke that string to select a pair of college center fielders and then returned to the college pitching well for the next three picks. They didn't draft a high schooler until their 12th pick. Led by Singer, four of those pitchers (Jackson Kowar, Brady Lynch, Kris Bubic) are represented in the Royals' top 10 prospects, and Lynch and Bubic were instrumental in Lexington's title run.

The plan, it seems, is to inject the college draftees into a system where most of the talent resides in the bottom half. Add quantity to the quality that already exists. There are no sure things in prospecting, so hedge your bets and stock more high-upside prospects into your system. It just might work. Maybe this can accelerate the timetable of The Process 2.0. Moore, who once proclaimed that good decisions could accelerate a five-year plan into a three-year plan while bad decisions could turn a ten-year plan into no plan, is understandably hesitant to place a timetable on exactly when these Royals could return to relevance. From a strategic standpoint, it makes sense to manage expectations.

This is where the Royals front office ran afoul during their first rebuild. Nobody in Kansas City pines for the days of Jose Guillen, right fielder. Instead, Moore provides markers and suggested milestones. The plan for the next couple of years will be to shed expensive contracts while restocking the farm system. If it walks like a rebuild and talks like a rebuild, it's probably a rebuild. The problem is the bad contracts are so awful that it won't be easy to find willing partners to deal. The potential upside of gaining a decent prospect in exchange for someone like Kennedy comes with a more realistic downside in which the Royals would have to sweeten the offer by including a young, cost-controlled player of their own just to rid themselves of an odious contract. One step forward while taking two steps back is no way to gain ground.

Instead, Moore points to 2021 as the year where The Process 2.0 will come into clearer focus. By then, the Royals will have separated the wheat from the chaff of this current prospect crop and they will be clear of the heaviest of their financial obligations. The team will presumably lose plenty of games in the meantime, so they will have the advantage of high draft picks and the bonus pool that goes with those. It also means at least two more years of not-rebuilding.

⚾ ⚾ ⚾

A funny thing happened down the stretch last summer: The Royals started winning, finishing the season by going 20-14. This coincided with the arrival of Adalberto Mondesi, who finally appeared ready to live up to the prospect expectations that have orbited around him since signing as a 16-year-old out of the Dominican Republic. The less unheralded Ryan O'Hearn got a late-season call-up and smashed 12 dingers in 170 plate appearances after homering only 11 times in Triple-A. They combined with Whit Merrifield—who at age 30 is the Royals' best player and most attractive trade chip—at the top of the order to bring back fond memories of the "Keep The Line Moving" days. The pitching was a little better. The hitting was timely. It also ran parallel to what Moore said was a conscious decision to stop talking about the rebuild. One of these reasons is not like the other.

Beware the September paper tigers. The desire to drop payroll under $100 million is understandable given there's no sense in throwing good money after bad baseball. Still, they're not tanking! Things are not necessarily going to be worse than last year, but it's a stretch to see them being much better. This season will feel like last season, and judging by where the Royals' farm system stands, with the bulk of the talent in the lower minors, 2020 will be similar. They can avoid the word "rebuild" all they like, but that won't change the reality. The Process 2.0 is still in its infancy. It's going to be another long summer in Kansas City.

At least those flags remain just beyond the left field wall, still flying.

—*Craig Brown is an author of Baseball Prospectus.*

Part 2: Player Analysis

Jorge Bonifacio RF
Born: 06/04/93 Age: 26 Bats: R Throws: R
Height: 6'1" Weight: 225 Origin: International Free Agent, 2009

YEAR	TEAM	LVL	AGE	PA	R	2B	3B	HR	RBI	BB	K	SB	CS	AVG/OBP/SLG
2016	OMA	AAA	23	558	82	22	6	19	86	51	130	6	2	.277/.351/.461
2017	OMA	AAA	24	57	6	2	2	3	12	6	8	0	0	.314/.386/.608
2017	KCA	MLB	24	422	55	15	1	17	40	35	118	1	1	.255/.320/.432
2018	OMA	AAA	25	58	11	5	1	0	9	7	12	0	0	.392/.466/.529
2018	KCA	MLB	25	270	31	16	2	4	23	29	71	0	1	.225/.312/.360
2019	KCA	MLB	26	423	47	17	2	13	48	37	107	1	1	.237/.308/.395

Breakout: 14% Improve: 46% Collapse: 4% Attrition: 17% MLB: 88%
Comparables: Josh Reddick, Brandon Moss, Corey Hart

The 2018 Royals posed the riddle: You have three outfield positions, but only fourth and fifth outfielders on your roster—what do you do? Part of the answer involved another long look at Bonifacio, who gave cause for encouragement with a 2017 season that held glimmers of promise. After an 80-game PED suspension nixed the first half of 2018, Bonifacio failed to impress in the second half, swiping the mantle of "Most Disappointing Outfield Jorge" from teammate Soler. On the brighter side, the Royals can certainly afford to dole out second (and third) chances, and the thin gruel of improving walk and strikeout rates may be enough to feed visions of mid-20s growth for Georgie Good Face.

YEAR	TEAM	LVL	AGE	PA	DRC+	VORP	BABIP	BRR	FRAA	WARP
2016	OMA	AAA	23	558	116	29.3	.339	1.2	RF(72): 13.8, LF(50): 7.0	3.4
2017	OMA	AAA	24	57	132	3.9	.325	-0.9	RF(9): 0.1, LF(3): 0.0	0.2
2017	KCA	MLB	24	422	101	5.3	.324	-0.1	RF(92): -9.9, LF(9): -0.5	-0.1
2018	OMA	AAA	25	58	158	5.4	.513	-0.2	RF(13): -1.2	0.3
2018	KCA	MLB	25	270	84	2.1	.301	0.0	RF(55): -0.8, LF(7): -1.0	-0.1
2019	KCA	MLB	26	423	93	6.8	.296	-0.5	RF -2, LF 0	0.4

Jorge Bonifacio, continued

Batted Ball Distribution

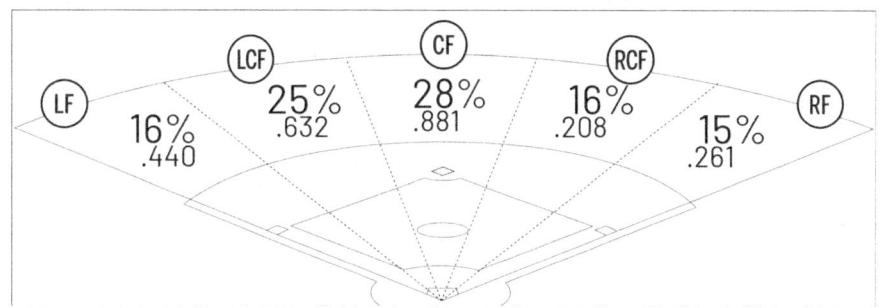

| | Strike Zone vs LHP | Strike Zone vs RHP |

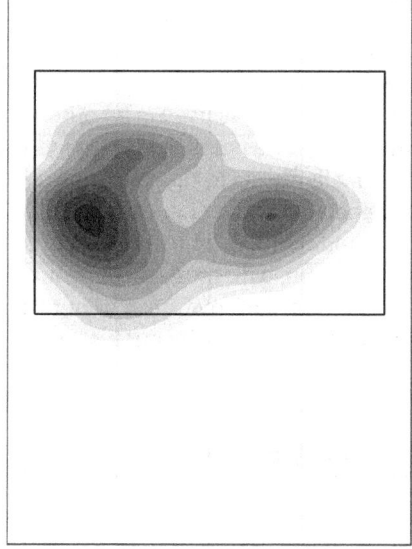

Kansas City Royals 2019

Cheslor Cuthbert 3B
Born: 11/16/92   Age: 26   Bats: R   Throws: R
Height: 6'1"   Weight: 210   Origin: International Free Agent, 2009

YEAR	TEAM	LVL	AGE	PA	R	2B	3B	HR	RBI	BB	K	SB	CS	AVG/OBP/SLG
2016	OMA	AAA	23	107	15	4	1	7	28	11	14	0	1	.333/.402/.624
2016	KCA	MLB	23	510	49	28	1	12	46	32	96	2	0	.274/.318/.413
2017	OMA	AAA	24	68	10	3	1	4	9	7	11	0	0	.271/.353/.559
2017	KCA	MLB	24	153	10	7	0	2	18	9	39	0	0	.231/.275/.322
2018	KCA	MLB	25	117	11	2	0	3	7	11	23	0	1	.194/.282/.301
2019	KCA	MLB	26	70	7	3	0	2	8	5	14	0	0	.250/.314/.391

Breakout: 11%   Improve: 55%   Collapse: 6%   Attrition: 18%   MLB: 95%
Comparables: Willy Aybar, Matt Duffy, Wilmer Flores

A news item that may have escaped mainstream notice: shortly after the conclusion of the 2018 regular season, Royals GM Dayton Moore wrote a formal request to MLB Commissioner Rob Manfred "to retire the position of third base for the Kansas City Royals organization, such that the team will no longer have the responsibility of covering that position for the remainder of time that the franchise remains active in Major League Baseball." The irredeemable fall from the greatness of George Brett, and the okay-ness of Mike Moustakas, were cited in the request. The somewhat informal phrasing "have you even seen our org depth chart?!" was used in an otherwise blandly bureaucratic document. When that request was (unsurprisingly) rejected, Brett himself was called, Moore probing lightly as to the question of his physical fitness in a potential age-66 comeback season. A perfunctory search of the Rolodex for Mark Teahen's agent was conducted. Hunter Dozier reluctantly began taking grounders at the hot corner again, with mutterings about (expletive) Ryan (expletive) O'Hearn and "that was *my* job" overheard. For three days, Moore felt uneasy. He felt like he had forgotten where he put his keys, or temporarily blanked on his Social Security number. Then it came to him. "Cuthbert. We've still got Cuthbert, right?" He sighed audibly. "Yep, I guess we've still got Cuthbert."

YEAR	TEAM	LVL	AGE	PA	DRC+	VORP	BABIP	BRR	FRAA	WARP
2016	OMA	AAA	23	107	175	14.8	.324	-1.4	3B(21): -2.0, 1B(3): 0.0	0.7
2016	KCA	MLB	23	510	94	5.9	.320	-5.1	3B(127): -2.1	0.7
2017	OMA	AAA	24	68	111	4.8	.267	0.0	3B(10): 0.6, 1B(2): -0.2	0.2
2017	KCA	MLB	24	153	77	-1.7	.301	0.2	3B(44): 0.6, 1B(6): 0.0	0.1
2018	KCA	MLB	25	117	88	-3.7	.218	0.6	3B(12): 0.1, 1B(10): -0.9	0.1
2019	KCA	MLB	26	70	96	0.6	.290	-0.1	1B -1	0.0

Cheslor Cuthbert, continued

Batted Ball Distribution

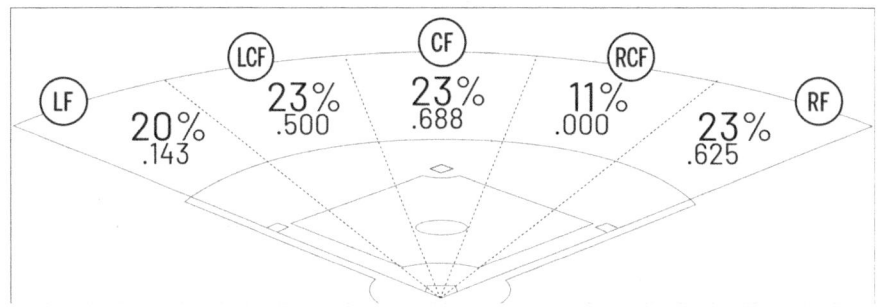

Strike Zone vs LHP   Strike Zone vs RHP

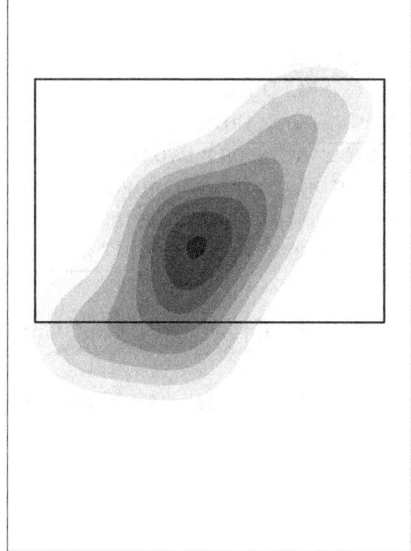

Hunter Dozier 1B

Born: 08/22/91 Age: 27 Bats: R Throws: R
Height: 6'4" Weight: 220 Origin: Round 1, 2013 Draft (#8 overall)

YEAR	TEAM	LVL	AGE	PA	R	2B	3B	HR	RBI	BB	K	SB	CS	AVG/OBP/SLG
2016	NWA	AA	24	110	14	8	0	8	21	14	23	4	0	.305/.400/.642
2016	OMA	AAA	24	434	65	36	1	15	54	40	100	3	1	.294/.357/.506
2016	KCA	MLB	24	21	4	1	0	0	1	2	8	0	0	.211/.286/.263
2017	OMA	AAA	25	96	11	6	1	4	12	9	37	1	1	.226/.313/.464
2018	OMA	AAA	26	143	18	7	0	1	11	24	43	2	1	.254/.385/.339
2018	KCA	MLB	26	388	36	19	4	11	34	24	109	2	3	.229/.278/.395
2019	KCA	MLB	27	556	57	29	3	15	62	46	157	4	2	.227/.294/.386

Breakout: 6% Improve: 29% Collapse: 11% Attrition: 23% MLB: 55%
Comparables: Jeff Baker, Mike Carp, Mark Canha

On February 4, 2017, Dozier posted a video to his Instagram account. You've seen these before, especially with baseball players: his partner tosses a plastic ball filled with colored powder, either pink or blue, indicating the biological sex of their unborn child. Amanda, his wife, gives him an underhand toss a bit inside, but Dozier keeps his hands in and squares up, the ball exploding blue powder. The first comment on the post, from "nsyndergaard": "Surprised you didn't whiff." Dozier and Thor are friends, but sometimes our pals can hide hard truths in levity: Dozier has run K rates around 30 percent across Triple-A and the majors over the past two seasons, and this, along with marginal defense, is keeping him from assuming the third-base mantle of the Moose. This season promises an opportunity—perhaps the final one—for Dozier to make memories on the baseball diamond that will be favorited beyond his circle of family and friends.

YEAR	TEAM	LVL	AGE	PA	DRC+	VORP	BABIP	BRR	FRAA	WARP
2016	NWA	AA	24	110	178	14.5	.328	0.1	3B(19): -0.3, LF(6): -1.2	0.8
2016	OMA	AAA	24	434	132	31.6	.358	0.9	3B(63): -6.6, RF(14): 1.0	1.3
2016	KCA	MLB	24	21	63	-0.2	.364	0.0	RF(7): -0.2	-0.1
2017	OMA	AAA	25	96	73	4.0	.341	-0.3	RF(10): -0.1, 3B(7): -0.3	-0.3
2018	OMA	AAA	26	143	115	5.4	.392	-0.2	3B(19): 0.6, RF(13): 1.2	0.6
2018	KCA	MLB	26	388	80	-4.7	.296	-0.3	1B(51): -7.5, 3B(37): -5.9	-1.5
2019	KCA	MLB	27	556	87	4.8	.298	-0.7	3B -9, 1B -2	-0.8

Hunter Dozier, continued

Batted Ball Distribution

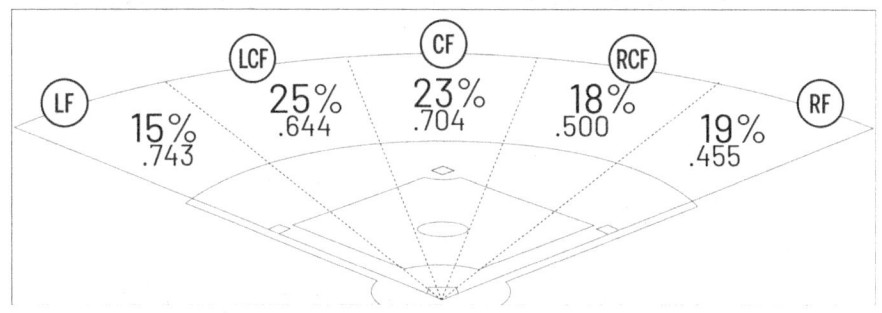

Strike Zone vs LHP **Strike Zone vs RHP**

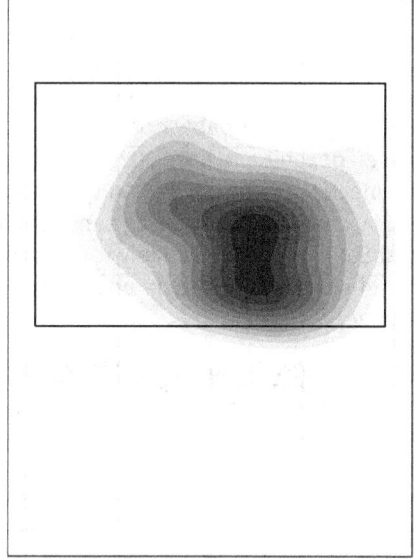

Kansas City Royals 2019

Cameron Gallagher C
Born: 12/06/92 Age: 26 Bats: R Throws: R
Height: 6'3" Weight: 230 Origin: Round 2, 2011 Draft (#65 overall)

YEAR	TEAM	LVL	AGE	PA	R	2B	3B	HR	RBI	BB	K	SB	CS	AVG/OBP/SLG
2016	NWA	AA	23	346	23	16	1	4	24	37	52	2	2	.259/.348/.359
2017	OMA	AAA	24	282	26	13	0	5	37	18	33	0	1	.292/.336/.400
2017	KCA	MLB	24	27	2	1	0	1	5	3	4	0	0	.250/.333/.417
2018	OMA	AAA	25	303	28	13	0	4	42	26	38	1	0	.265/.334/.358
2018	KCA	MLB	25	69	5	3	0	1	7	3	15	0	0	.206/.250/.302
2019	KCA	MLB	26	244	23	9	1	6	26	15	41	0	0	.237/.288/.366

Breakout: 10% Improve: 32% Collapse: 5% Attrition: 17% MLB: 49%
Comparables: Jordan Pacheco, Sandy Leon, Bruce Maxwell

You've got a reliable old truck that you seldom use except for that trip to the dump every few months, or when your buddy needs to move that absurdly heavy sofabed across town. You've been happy with your everyday car, and it starts pretty much every time you turn the key; you'll replace it someday, but probably not for a few years (after all, your contract—er, lease—doesn't end until 2021). The thing about your truck: it'll get you where you need to go, but man, you really thought it had more power. I mean, the ol' jalopy couldn't even manage an ISO over .100 in the hitter-friendly PCL. Given that Sal Perez was less likely to break down than this extended metaphor, at least before he did, the defense-only Gallagher is now an acceptable backup vehicle to a loaner.

YEAR	TEAM	P. COUNT	FRM RUNS	BLK RUNS	THRW RUNS	TOT RUNS
2017	KCA	1026	-0.2	0.2	-0.1	0.6
2017	OMA	9981	11.1	1.6	1.0	14.1
2018	KCA	2387	1.5	1.0	0.0	2.6
2018	OMA	9812	11.3	0.3	0.1	11.4
2019	KCA	9096	5.3	0.9	0.0	6.3

YEAR	TEAM	LVL	AGE	PA	DRC+	VORP	BABIP	BRR	FRAA	WARP
2016	NWA	AA	23	346	108	11.1	.300	-3.9	C(80): 17.0	2.5
2017	OMA	AAA	24	282	94	5.5	.317	-4.1	C(71): 11.8	1.6
2017	KCA	MLB	24	27	93	0.4	.263	-0.4	C(13): -0.2	0.0
2018	OMA	AAA	25	303	85	11.3	.294	-2.0	C(72): 11.9	1.5
2018	KCA	MLB	25	69	84	-1.9	.250	-1.6	C(20): 2.4	0.3
2019	KCA	MLB	26	244	64	0.5	.263	-0.4	C 4	0.3

Cameron Gallagher, continued

Batted Ball Distribution

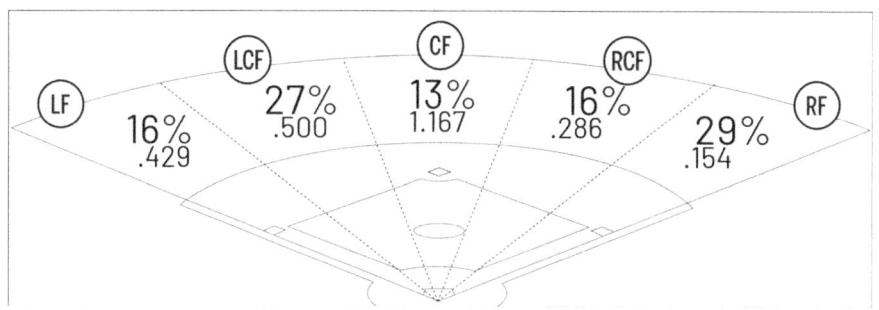

Strike Zone vs LHP **Strike Zone vs RHP**

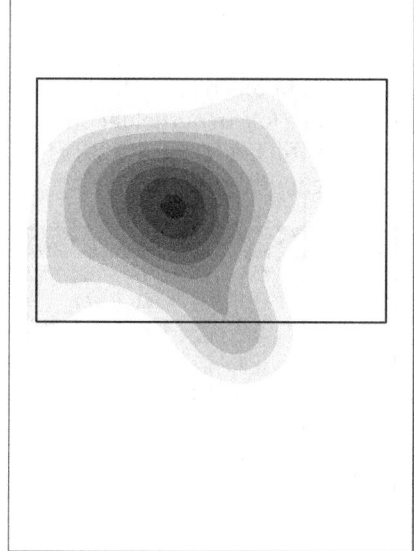

Brian Goodwin OF

Born: 11/02/90 Age: 28 Bats: L Throws: R
Height: 6'0" Weight: 200 Origin: Round 1, 2011 Draft (#34 overall)

YEAR	TEAM	LVL	AGE	PA	R	2B	3B	HR	RBI	BB	K	SB	CS	AVG/OBP/SLG
2016	SYR	AAA	25	492	51	25	1	14	68	46	106	15	3	.280/.349/.438
2016	WAS	MLB	25	44	1	4	1	0	5	2	14	0	0	.286/.318/.429
2017	SYR	AAA	26	103	9	4	0	2	11	10	29	2	1	.256/.327/.367
2017	WAS	MLB	26	278	41	21	1	13	30	23	69	6	0	.251/.313/.498
2018	WAS	MLB	27	79	9	1	0	3	12	10	26	3	1	.200/.321/.354
2018	OMA	AAA	27	44	6	4	0	2	9	4	11	0	0	.225/.295/.475
2018	KCA	MLB	27	101	11	5	0	3	13	6	31	1	1	.266/.317/.415
2019	KCA	MLB	28	184	21	9	1	5	20	14	47	3	1	.234/.295/.389

Breakout: 3% Improve: 43% Collapse: 16% Attrition: 28% MLB: 88%
Comparables: Ryan Church, Kirk Nieuwenhuis, Scott Hairston

So maybe Goodwin's mid-season trade to Kansas City didn't result in his raising his outstretched arms in the driving rain, *Shawshank*-style. But getting out of Washington's deep outfield and onto a team where opportunity abounds had to feel liberating for the former first-round pick. Goodwin held his own in his brief Royals debut, but as has been the case throughout his career, the swing-and-miss in his approach mitigates his power/speed upside. A fifth outfielder on a good team, a fourth outfielder on an average team, Goodwin projects to be the starting center fielder for the 2019 Royals, and perhaps beyond, depending on how the rebuild fares.

YEAR	TEAM	LVL	AGE	PA	DRC+	VORP	BABIP	BRR	FRAA	WARP
2016	SYR	AAA	25	492	121	21.3	.336	-2.1	CF(85): -4.9, RF(18): 0.3	1.5
2016	WAS	MLB	25	44	69	0.4	.429	-0.2	RF(8): -1.5, LF(5): -0.3	-0.3
2017	SYR	AAA	26	103	92	0.4	.350	-1.6	RF(9): 0.8, CF(8): 0.0	-0.1
2017	WAS	MLB	26	278	97	13.2	.291	0.1	CF(34): -1.2, LF(31): -0.2	0.8
2018	WAS	MLB	27	79	80	-0.6	.270	-1.8	LF(11): -0.2, RF(10): -0.7	-0.2
2018	OMA	AAA	27	44	89	2.6	.259	0.1	CF(3): -0.5, LF(2): 0.9	0.0
2018	KCA	MLB	27	101	84	3.6	.367	0.2	CF(25): -0.7, LF(1): -0.1	0.1
2019	KCA	MLB	28	184	87	3.3	.290	0.2	CF -2, RF 0	0.1

Brian Goodwin, continued

Batted Ball Distribution

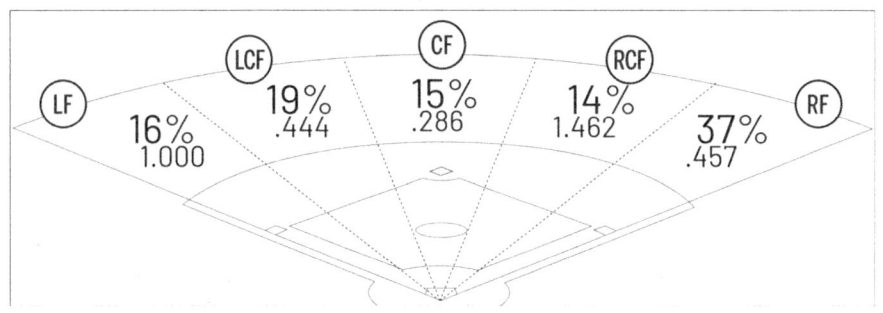

Strike Zone vs LHP   **Strike Zone vs RHP**

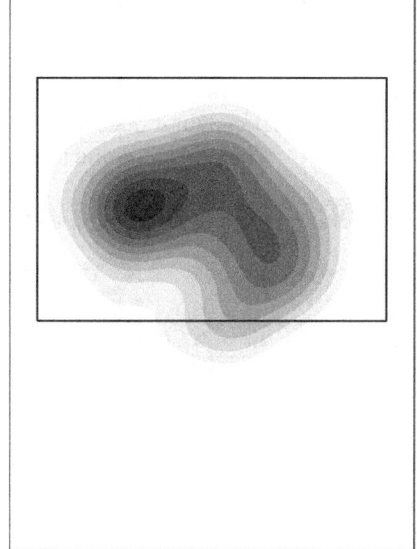

Alex Gordon LF

Born: 02/10/84 Age: 35 Bats: L Throws: R
Height: 6'1" Weight: 225 Origin: Round 1, 2005 Draft (#2 overall)

YEAR	TEAM	LVL	AGE	PA	R	2B	3B	HR	RBI	BB	K	SB	CS	AVG/OBP/SLG
2016	KCA	MLB	32	506	62	16	2	17	40	52	148	8	1	.220/.312/.380
2017	KCA	MLB	33	541	52	20	2	9	45	45	126	7	4	.208/.293/.315
2018	KCA	MLB	34	568	56	24	0	13	54	50	124	12	2	.245/.324/.370
2019	KCA	MLB	35	526	56	22	2	10	48	47	125	8	3	.228/.312/.348

Breakout: 1% Improve: 24% Collapse: 14% Attrition: 25% MLB: 68%
Comparables: Kevin McReynolds, Jason Michaels, Rube Bressler

Baseball analysts always talk of the uneven developmental curve of prospects. We know that growth is anything but linear, with so many variables in play: changes in bodily composition, the increased difficulty of ascending levels, the acquisition of new skills or the significant improvement of existing ones. What often goes unnoticed is the uneven decline curve of major-leaguers; the Grim Reaper comes for us all, but sometimes he takes a coffee break between gathering our mortal coils. There's no question that Gordon is in decline—his yearly WARP had been plummeting since his 2011-14 peak—but he found a tiny ledge on the cliff in 2018, getting to double digits in both homers and steals and recording a WARP that was no longer in red ink. None of this portends a late-career renaissance, but it does make it slightly more palatable for the Royals to shell out $20 million for that one final hit of championship-era nostalgia.

YEAR	TEAM	LVL	AGE	PA	DRC+	VORP	BABIP	BRR	FRAA	WARP
2016	KCA	MLB	32	506	91	1.6	.288	1.2	LF(126): -3.1	0.5
2017	KCA	MLB	33	541	69	-8.8	.261	-0.2	LF(140): 2.7, CF(15): -0.9	-0.5
2018	KCA	MLB	34	568	90	4.3	.299	-1.9	LF(125): 3.3, CF(11): -0.9	0.8
2019	KCA	MLB	35	526	83	4.6	.288	0.1	LF 1	0.5

Alex Gordon, continued

Batted Ball Distribution

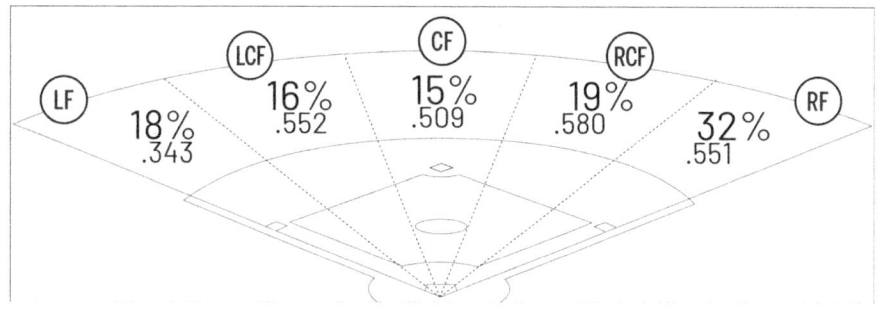

Strike Zone vs LHP

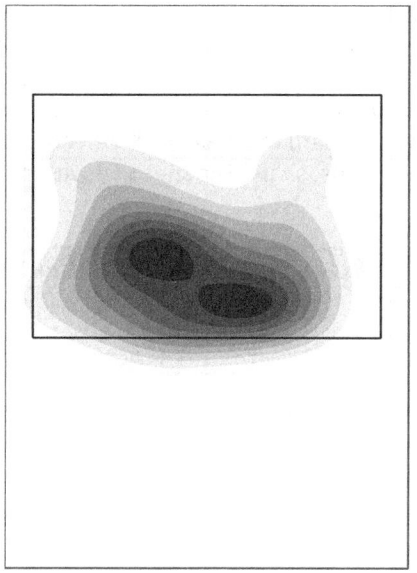

Strike Zone vs RHP

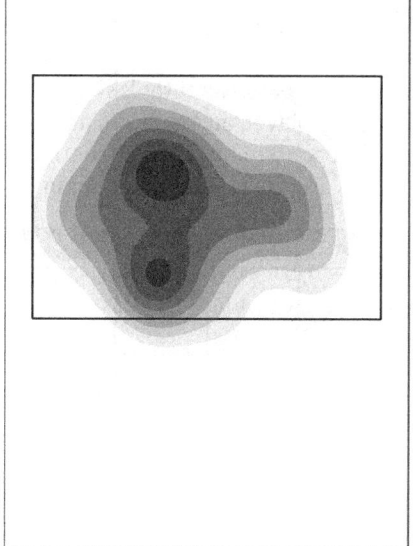

Billy Hamilton CF

Born: 09/09/90 Age: 28 Bats: B Throws: R
Height: 6'0" Weight: 160 Origin: Round 2, 2009 Draft (#57 overall)

YEAR	TEAM	LVL	AGE	PA	R	2B	3B	HR	RBI	BB	K	SB	CS	AVG/OBP/SLG
2016	CIN	MLB	25	460	69	19	3	3	17	36	93	58	8	.260/.321/.343
2017	CIN	MLB	26	633	85	17	11	4	38	44	133	59	13	.247/.299/.335
2018	CIN	MLB	27	556	74	16	9	4	29	46	132	34	10	.236/.299/.327
2019	KCA	MLB	28	417	52	16	5	4	31	30	88	35	8	.247/.304/.348

Breakout: 11% Improve: 50% Collapse: 9% Attrition: 25% MLB: 94%
Comparables: Willy Taveras, Chuck Carr, Lance Johnson

No player of recent vintage has made such modest contributions to winning a baseball game as scintillating as Hamilton. Few things on the diamond can match the excitement of watching him chase down a gapper with runners on base or dash first-to-third in a seeming heartbeat. In some ways his anemic bat makes him more of an entertainer than a ballplayer, and as fans and analysts ruminate over the effect fewer balls in play have on the game's appeal, keep in mind that players like Hamilton are the ones most affected. Fewer fly balls mean fewer opportunities to add value by hauling them in; more strikeouts and home runs mean getting to second or third base are less important to scoring runs than in the past. Hamilton's skill set is becoming less and less viable for an everyday player, and MLB will need to do some hard thinking on whether or not that is a good thing. In the meantime, hello, Kansas City! The speed, glove, and out-making ways should fit right in.

YEAR	TEAM	LVL	AGE	PA	DRC+	VORP	BABIP	BRR	FRAA	WARP
2016	CIN	MLB	25	460	72	13.4	.329	10.5	CF(115): 9.5	2.0
2017	CIN	MLB	26	633	66	4.7	.313	6.6	CF(137): 5.1	0.7
2018	CIN	MLB	27	556	70	8.2	.309	8.3	CF(150): 4.2	1.2
2019	KCA	MLB	28	417	76	9.4	.303	5.5	CF 0	0.9

Billy Hamilton, continued

Batted Ball Distribution

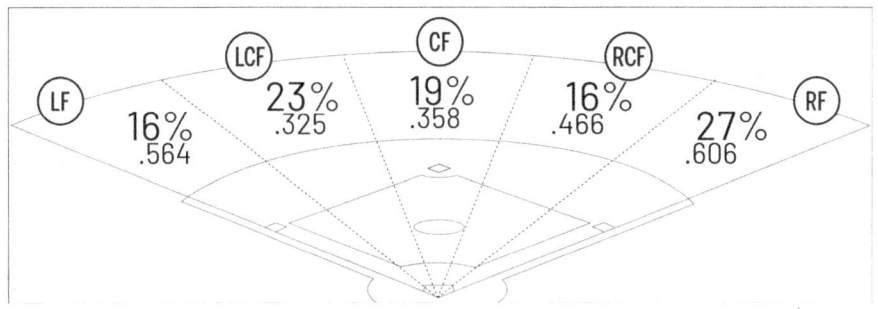

Strike Zone vs LHP   Strike Zone vs RHP

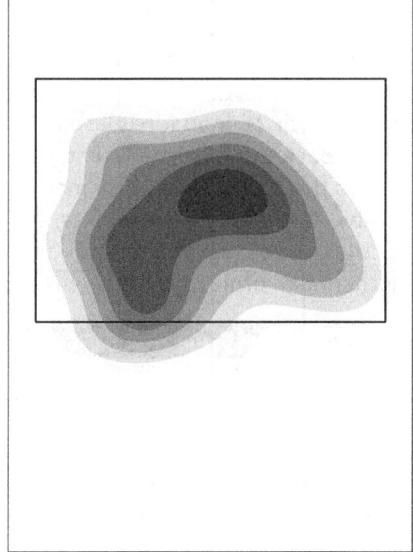

Martin Maldonado C

Born: 08/16/86 Age: 32 Bats: R Throws: R
Height: 6'0" Weight: 230 Origin: Round 27, 2004 Draft (#803 overall)

YEAR	TEAM	LVL	AGE	PA	R	2B	3B	HR	RBI	BB	K	SB	CS	AVG/OBP/SLG
2016	MIL	MLB	29	253	21	7	0	8	21	35	56	1	0	.202/.332/.351
2017	ANA	MLB	30	471	43	19	1	14	38	15	119	0	2	.221/.276/.368
2018	ANA	MLB	31	290	24	14	0	5	32	13	73	0	1	.223/.284/.332
2018	HOU	MLB	31	114	15	4	1	4	12	3	25	0	0	.231/.257/.398
2019	KCA	MLB	32	362	38	14	1	9	37	30	82	1	1	.227/.312/.363

Breakout: 2%   Improve: 42%   Collapse: 16%   Attrition: 17%   MLB: 98%
Comparables: Al Evans, Matt Wieters, Hank Deberry

YEAR	TEAM	P. COUNT	FRM RUNS	BLK RUNS	THRW RUNS	TOT RUNS
2016	MIL	9275	2.5	1.3	2.1	7.5
2017	ANA	18609	27.2	1.0	3.2	32.0
2018	ANA	11256	4.1	-0.8	0.3	4.0
2018	HOU	4686	1.7	-0.3	0.2	2.6
2019	KCA	14156	9.3	0.3	1.6	11.2

Comedian Lewis Black had a joke long ago regarding being a weather reporter in San Diego, California, and how it was easily the best job in the country since all one had to do every day was proclaim "It's going to be nice. Back to you." While writing about Martin Maldonado full time would not put even the meagerest portion of bread on a table, the temptation is hard to resist: "Martin Maldonado is a solid defensive catcher who struggles to hit his weight. Back to you." Except that, entering his age-32 season, there's legitimate concern that the solid defense may be slipping away; framing may seem invisible, but it requires flexibility, and at some point a man can't just pluck those low strikes up with the same level of grace. I guess the point is that even in Southern California, the weather reporter is wrong once in a while.

YEAR	TEAM	LVL	AGE	PA	DRC+	VORP	BABIP	BRR	FRAA	WARP
2016	MIL	MLB	29	253	91	6.5	.234	-1.1	C(69): 5.5	1.4
2017	ANA	MLB	30	471	73	2.0	.273	-2.4	C(137): 32.1, 1B(1): 0.0	3.8
2018	ANA	MLB	31	290	74	3.2	.287	-0.1	C(77): 1.1	0.6
2018	HOU	MLB	31	114	75	-0.3	.263	-0.6	C(40): 2.0	0.4
2019	KCA	MLB	32	362	88	10.8	.277	-0.7	C 9	1.9

Martin Maldonado, continued

Batted Ball Distribution

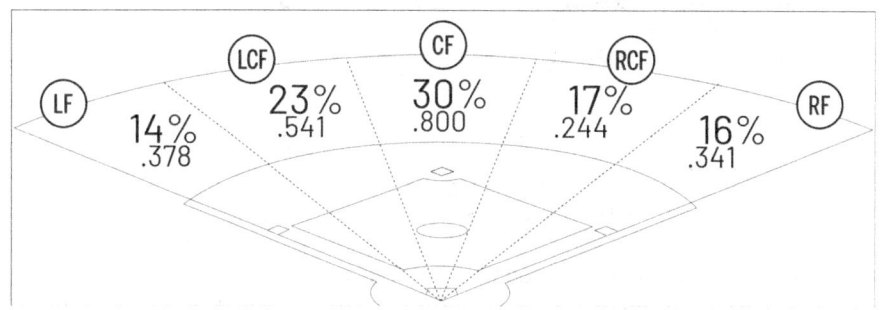

Strike Zone vs LHP

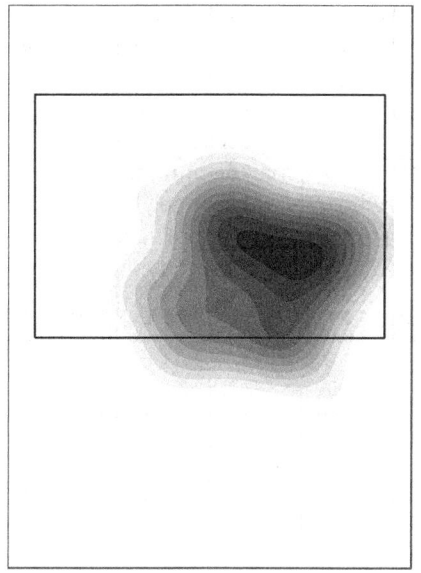

Strike Zone vs RHP

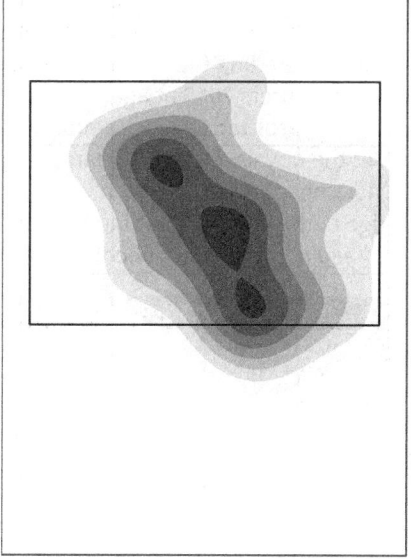

Kansas City Royals 2019

Whit Merrifield 2B
Born: 01/24/89 Age: 30 Bats: R Throws: R
Height: 6'0" Weight: 195 Origin: Round 9, 2010 Draft (#269 overall)

YEAR	TEAM	LVL	AGE	PA	R	2B	3B	HR	RBI	BB	K	SB	CS	AVG/OBP/SLG
2016	OMA	AAA	27	304	46	19	0	8	29	22	55	20	2	.266/.321/.423
2016	KCA	MLB	27	332	44	22	3	2	29	19	72	8	3	.283/.323/.392
2017	KCA	MLB	28	630	80	32	6	19	78	29	88	34	8	.288/.324/.460
2018	KCA	MLB	29	707	88	43	3	12	60	61	114	45	10	.304/.367/.438
2019	KCA	MLB	30	623	88	34	4	15	60	45	105	32	8	.277/.335/.431

Breakout: 7%   Improve: 42%   Collapse: 4%   Attrition: 4%   MLB: 92%
Comparables: Freddy Sanchez, Josh Harrison, Mike Aviles

While it's true that one indeed can't spell "Whit" without "hit"—a category in which Merrifield improbably finished tops in the AL—it's equally true that one can't spell "Whit" without "WTH," as in, what the H-E-double-hockey-sticks happened to turn a low-ceiling org soldier into a four-win, black-ink-owning, bona fide star? Maybe we lay a bit of the power spike at the juicy baseball of 2017, but Merrifield has excelled in non-power aspects as well: he's improved his walk rates, he hits effectively to all fields, and he's stealing bases frequently and efficiently (leading the AL for two years running). Given his late blooming, Merrifield enters 2019 at age 30 with one more year at the league minimum before the arbitration clock starts, so the questions he poses are questions about the Royals' future writ large: hold at low cost, making him the cornerstone through the lean years; extend with a long-term deal, building a bridge to the next contending team and a face for the fans; or cash out via trade and keep filling the prospect tank? What does one do with found money?

YEAR	TEAM	LVL	AGE	PA	DRC+	VORP	BABIP	BRR	FRAA	WARP
2016	OMA	AAA	27	304	103	14.4	.302	1.5	2B(40): 1.5, LF(9): -0.6	0.5
2016	KCA	MLB	27	332	87	6.0	.361	-0.2	2B(65): 2.2, LF(13): 1.9	0.9
2017	KCA	MLB	28	630	113	26.8	.308	1.7	2B(132): -0.2, RF(10): -1.9	2.9
2018	KCA	MLB	29	707	119	38.9	.352	3.5	2B(108): 2.3, CF(30): 1.4	4.4
2019	KCA	MLB	30	623	107	28.7	.313	3.8	2B 2, RF -1	3.2

Whit Merrifield, continued

Batted Ball Distribution

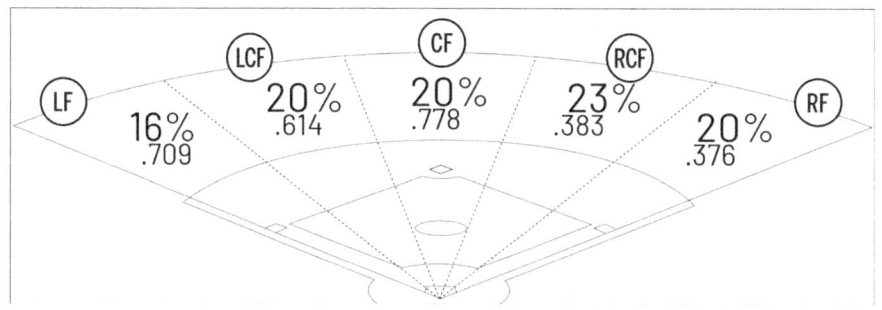

Strike Zone vs LHP   **Strike Zone vs RHP**

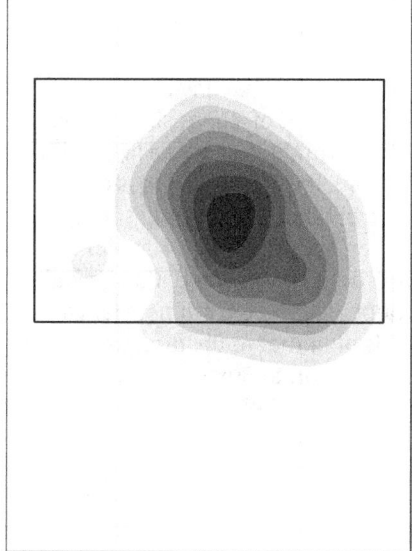

Kansas City Royals 2019

Adalberto Mondesi SS
Born: 07/27/95   Age: 23   Bats: B   Throws: R
Height: 6'1"   Weight: 190   Origin: International Free Agent, 2011

YEAR	TEAM	LVL	AGE	PA	R	2B	3B	HR	RBI	BB	K	SB	CS	AVG/OBP/SLG
2016	WIL	A+	20	39	5	2	1	1	4	2	11	2	0	.243/.282/.432
2016	NWA	AA	20	131	20	5	1	5	17	13	30	17	1	.259/.331/.448
2016	OMA	AAA	20	61	9	2	4	1	9	2	19	5	0	.304/.328/.536
2016	KCA	MLB	20	149	16	1	3	2	13	6	48	9	1	.185/.231/.281
2017	OMA	AAA	21	357	52	20	8	13	52	18	86	21	3	.305/.340/.539
2017	KCA	MLB	21	60	4	1	0	1	3	3	22	5	2	.170/.214/.245
2018	OMA	AAA	22	133	19	8	3	5	21	8	30	10	0	.250/.295/.492
2018	KCA	MLB	22	291	47	13	3	14	37	11	77	32	7	.276/.306/.498
2019	KCA	MLB	23	545	85	22	6	18	53	29	142	43	8	.241/.286/.418

Breakout: 24%   Improve: 62%   Collapse: 8%   Attrition: 15%   MLB: 88%
Comparables: Adam Jones, Hanley Ramirez, Chris Owings

For a team saved only by the historically dismal Orioles from being the worst in baseball, the second half of the Royals' season was surprisingly… not that depressing? The power explosion of Ryan O'Hearn, the quiet emergence of Brad Keller, and the burnishing of Whit Merrifield's excellence all made for good, happy stories. But any optimistic account of the Royals' 2018 has to begin with the breakout of Mondesi, who pulled a Joey/Albert Belle and proceeded to barnstorm the AL Central like an infield version of Byron Buxton (late 2017 edition). It was easy to gloss over the impatient plate approach when the eyes were blinded with blazing speed and surprising power. In the colder days of winter, a long, hard look at Mondesi's performance leaves a number of questions unanswered: Can he walk even just a bit more? The power was no doubt luck-driven, but how far will it regress? Is there a risk that the on-base skills plummet to the disastrous level of Buxton (2018 edition)? As the comparison to Buxton suggests, there's a natural pull for storylines to veer toward happy endings or darkest timelines. Reality tends to live between the poles, a region populated by uneven-but-productive players like Tim Anderson and Jonathan Villar. Prospects who flash star qualities usually won't end up being stars, and if Mondesi finds a home in the great, flawed middle, it will still count as a win for the Royals.

YEAR	TEAM	LVL	AGE	PA	DRC+	VORP	BABIP	BRR	FRAA	WARP
2016	WIL	A+	20	39	54	1.5	.320	0.9	SS(6): 0.5	0.0
2016	NWA	AA	20	131	116	10.5	.305	1.0	SS(21): 2.1, 2B(6): 0.4	0.8
2016	OMA	AAA	20	61	81	7.1	.444	1.4	SS(12): 0.6, 2B(2): 0.1	0.3
2016	KCA	MLB	20	149	49	-5.1	.271	1.5	2B(42): -4.4, SS(7): -0.1	-0.8
2017	OMA	AAA	21	357	110	31.3	.373	1.3	SS(71): 2.2, 2B(10): 0.1	1.9
2017	KCA	MLB	21	60	50	-5.8	.267	-1.4	2B(14): 0.1, SS(9): 0.1	-0.3
2018	OMA	AAA	22	133	74	7.6	.291	1.2	SS(18): 0.6, 2B(6): 0.8	0.2
2018	KCA	MLB	22	291	104	18.6	.335	0.3	SS(61): 1.2, 2B(12): 0.9	1.6
2019	KCA	MLB	23	545	86	13.2	.291	7.8	SS 5	2.4

Adalberto Mondesi, continued

Batted Ball Distribution

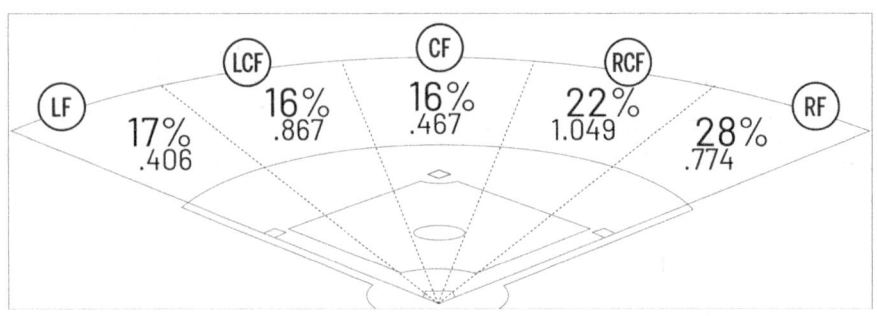

Strike Zone vs LHP   **Strike Zone vs RHP**

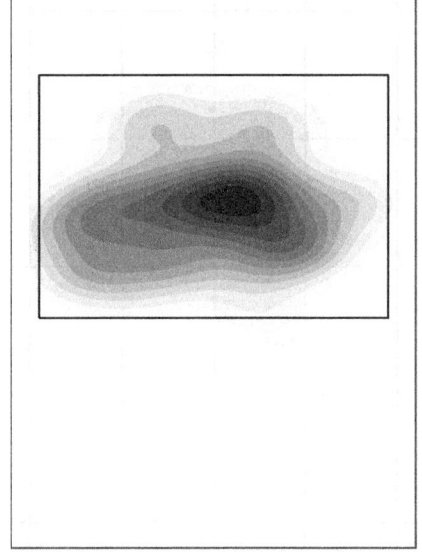

Ryan O'Hearn 1B

Born: 07/26/93 Age: 25 Bats: L Throws: L
Height: 6'3" Weight: 200 Origin: Round 8, 2014 Draft (#243 overall)

YEAR	TEAM	LVL	AGE	PA	R	2B	3B	HR	RBI	BB	K	SB	CS	AVG/OBP/SLG
2016	WIL	A+	22	98	13	7	0	7	18	8	27	0	0	.352/.408/.670
2016	NWA	AA	22	466	49	25	2	15	60	48	131	3	5	.258/.339/.437
2017	OMA	AAA	23	463	48	26	1	18	53	45	119	1	0	.252/.325/.450
2017	NWA	AA	23	76	7	1	1	4	11	10	20	0	0	.258/.355/.485
2018	OMA	AAA	24	406	47	21	1	11	52	45	97	2	0	.232/.322/.391
2018	KCA	MLB	24	170	23	10	2	12	30	20	45	0	0	.262/.353/.597
2019	KCA	MLB	25	529	57	24	2	19	65	50	137	0	0	.217/.294/.398

Breakout: 7% Improve: 28% Collapse: 4% Attrition: 21% MLB: 53%
Comparables: Travis Ishikawa, Brandon Allen, Tyler Austin

A lefty power bat, O'Hearn hit an underwhelming 11 home runs in 406 plate appearances at Triple-A Omaha. After a late-July call-up to Kansas City, he proceeded to hit 12 bombs in only 170 times under the lights. (And they say there's nothing different about the major-league ball.) O'Hearn has his obvious strengths, starting with his… well… strength. He also knows how to take a free pass, walking in around 12 percent of his plate appearances across both Triple-A and the majors. His weaknesses become apparent the moment you click on his splits: with a triple-slash of .108/.195/.270 against major-league lefties, you see the prototypical picture of a platoon first baseman. But there's a twist! O'Hearn's minor-league splits tilt the *other* way, so his first order of business in 2019 will be proving that he can handle major-league lefties. And if he can't, there's nothing wrong with being a strong-side platoon bat, provided the Royals don't fantasize about bigger things.

YEAR	TEAM	LVL	AGE	PA	DRC+	VORP	BABIP	BRR	FRAA	WARP
2016	WIL	A+	22	98	177	13.7	.436	-0.3	1B(21): -0.7	0.5
2016	NWA	AA	22	466	122	14.8	.342	-2.8	1B(61): 1.9, LF(39): -3.7	0.3
2017	OMA	AAA	23	463	96	5.2	.309	-2.5	1B(75): -1.2, RF(5): -0.2	-0.5
2017	NWA	AA	23	76	124	3.0	.310	0.1	1B(8): 0.3, LF(5): -0.6	0.1
2018	OMA	AAA	24	406	91	6.0	.286	3.9	1B(69): -6.3, LF(13): -2.1	-0.8
2018	KCA	MLB	24	170	130	9.0	.293	-3.6	1B(31): 0.4, LF(1): -0.1	0.5
2019	KCA	MLB	25	529	90	3.4	.261	-0.9	1B -3	0.0

Ryan O'Hearn, continued

Batted Ball Distribution

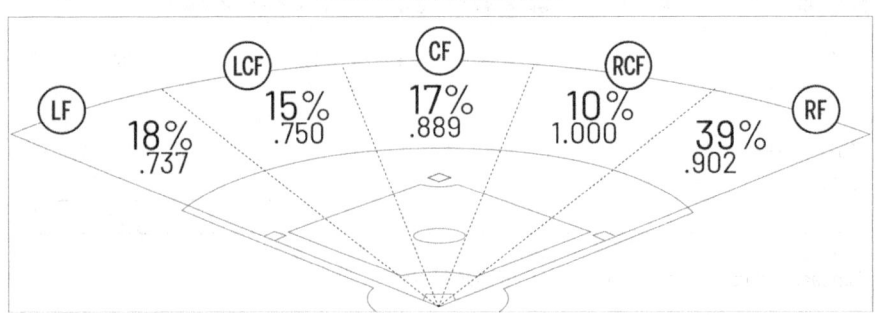

Strike Zone vs LHP   **Strike Zone vs RHP**

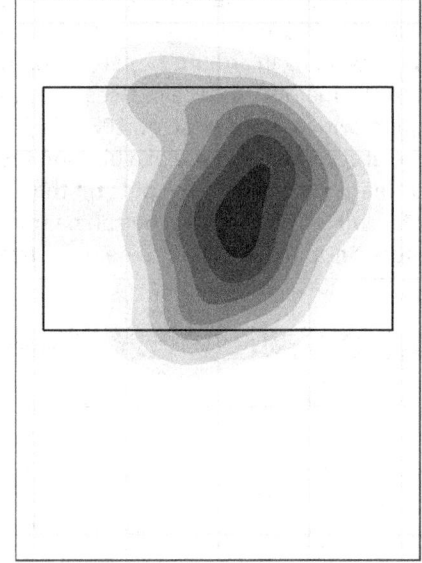

Chris Owings UT

Born: 08/12/91 Age: 27 Bats: R Throws: R
Height: 5'10" Weight: 185 Origin: Round 1, 2009 Draft (#41 overall)

YEAR	TEAM	LVL	AGE	PA	R	2B	3B	HR	RBI	BB	K	SB	CS	AVG/OBP/SLG
2016	ARI	MLB	24	466	52	24	11	5	49	20	87	21	2	.277/.315/.416
2017	ARI	MLB	25	386	41	25	1	12	51	17	87	12	2	.268/.299/.442
2018	RNO	AAA	26	92	15	4	2	1	11	1	17	1	2	.286/.293/.407
2018	ARI	MLB	26	309	34	15	0	4	22	24	75	11	4	.206/.272/.302
2019	KCA	MLB	27	340	37	16	2	7	34	21	72	12	3	.247/.299/.378

Breakout: 12% Improve: 43% Collapse: 13% Attrition: 27% MLB: 90%
Comparables: Mel Clark, Roman Mejias, Alex Ochoa

The Diamondbacks once seemed to choose Owings over Didi Gregorius. In their defense, Gregorius wasn't hitting yet and Owings was the sort of gritty, do-it-all, hard-nosed player coveted by the fallen regime of the past. That decision ultimately provided the opening seized by Nick Ahmed, leaving Owings on the outside looking in. Slowed by injuries and battling inconsistency, he assumed a super-utility role for 2018 but couldn't pass that test as he was dismal at the dish. Just 27, he moves on to an organization that always loves grit and gloves, inking a one-year deal with the Royals to replace Alcides Escobar.

YEAR	TEAM	LVL	AGE	PA	DRC+	VORP	BABIP	BRR	FRAA	WARP
2016	ARI	MLB	24	466	81	14.7	.334	1.9	SS(70): -3.5, CF(49): -1.9	0.4
2017	ARI	MLB	25	386	85	14.9	.318	-0.6	SS(54): 4.2, RF(25): 1.5	1.2
2018	RNO	AAA	26	92	64	-0.6	.342	1.4	2B(10): -0.2, 3B(6): 0.3	0.0
2018	ARI	MLB	26	309	70	-6.4	.265	0.8	RF(43): -1.1, CF(16): 1.2	-0.4
2019	KCA	MLB	27	340	86	5.3	.297	1.3	3B -1, 2B 1	0.6

Kansas City Royals 2019

Chris Owings, continued

Batted Ball Distribution

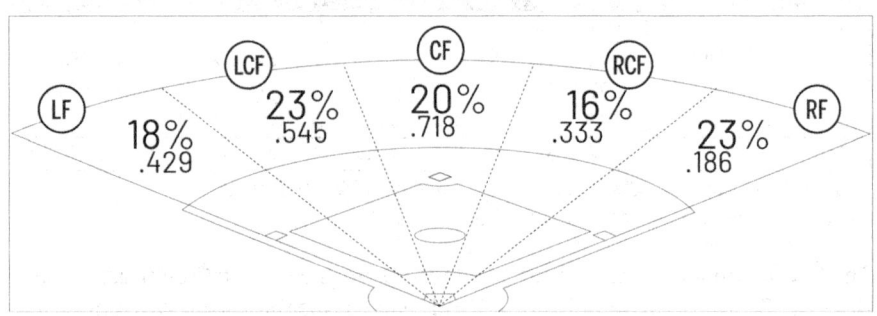

Strike Zone vs LHP   **Strike Zone vs RHP**

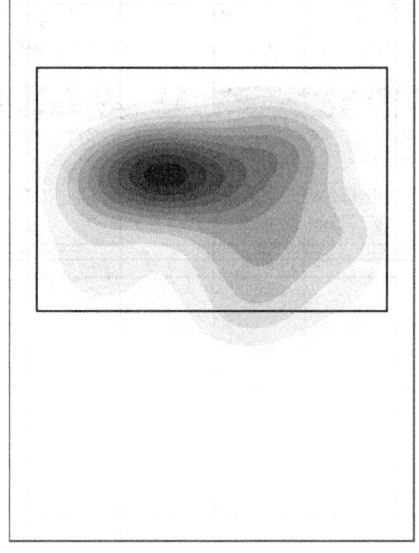

Salvador Perez   C

Born: 05/10/90   Age: 29   Bats: R   Throws: R
Height: 6'4"   Weight: 240   Origin: International Free Agent, 2006

YEAR	TEAM	LVL	AGE	PA	R	2B	3B	HR	RBI	BB	K	SB	CS	AVG/OBP/SLG
2016	KCA	MLB	26	546	57	28	2	22	64	22	119	0	0	.247/.288/.438
2017	KCA	MLB	27	499	57	24	1	27	80	17	95	1	0	.268/.297/.495
2018	KCA	MLB	28	544	52	23	0	27	80	17	108	1	1	.235/.274/.439
2019	KCA	MLB	29	509	59	26	2	22	72	29	101	1	0	.255/.309/.453

Breakout: 4%   Improve: 38%   Collapse: 14%   Attrition: 11%   MLB: 95%
Comparables: Wilson Ramos, Matt Nokes, Harry Danning

YEAR	TEAM	P. COUNT	FRM RUNS	BLK RUNS	THRW RUNS	TOT RUNS
2016	KCA	18379	-9.5	2.9	5.6	-1.4
2017	KCA	15629	-10.0	1.5	0.1	-8.4
2018	KCA	14052	-9.9	-0.6	0.8	-9.5
2019	KCA	16638	-12.5	1.3	1.7	-9.5

Perez will enter his ninth major-league season still not having blown out thirty candles. While teammate and relative major-league *arriviste* Whit Merrifield passed this magic milestone in January, the general sense of Salvy is that he long ago stepped out of a wagon train on the far edge of Missouri, gazed westward across the Kansas plains, donned his gear, and uttered: "Here. I will stay here." Perez and the Royals have been through a lot—futility, relevance, almost-championship, CHAMPIONSHIP, irrelevance, futility again—and Perez has played through nearly all of it, as he's one 2017 missed plate appearance from six straight seasons with at least 500. He's been around long enough that we know his strengths (durability, power, solid defense, charm) and weaknesses (won't take a walk, not a great framer, limits career opportunities of backup catchers). With a contract that keeps him in Kansas City through 2021, Perez represents the likeliest last link to the glory days of 2014-15. But for now his value to the club is still anchored in present value, rather than sepia-toned memories. Of course that present value is rendered moot for 2019, as Perez will miss the full length of the season after undergoing Tommy John surgery.

YEAR	TEAM	LVL	AGE	PA	DRC+	VORP	BABIP	BRR	FRAA	WARP
2016	KCA	MLB	26	546	97	12.7	.280	-2.7	C(128): -1.9, 1B(1): 0.0	1.9
2017	KCA	MLB	27	499	112	19.5	.280	-1.3	C(115): -10.2	1.9
2018	KCA	MLB	28	544	104	9.5	.245	-3.7	C(96): -8.1, 1B(3): 0.0	1.3
2019	KCA	MLB	29	509	106	24.0	.285	-2.1	C -10	1.5

Kansas City Royals 2019

Salvador Perez, continued

Batted Ball Distribution

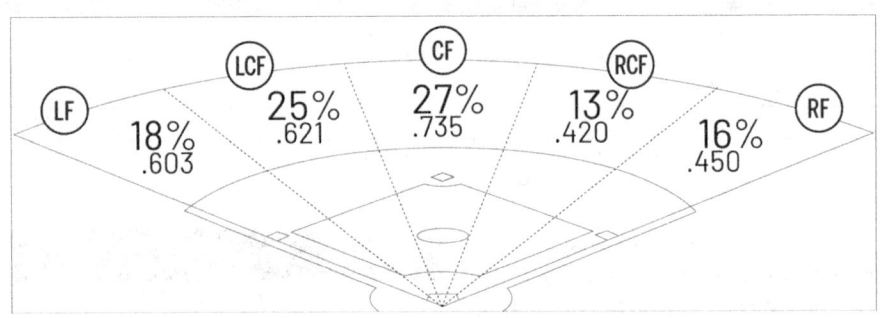

Strike Zone vs LHP   Strike Zone vs RHP

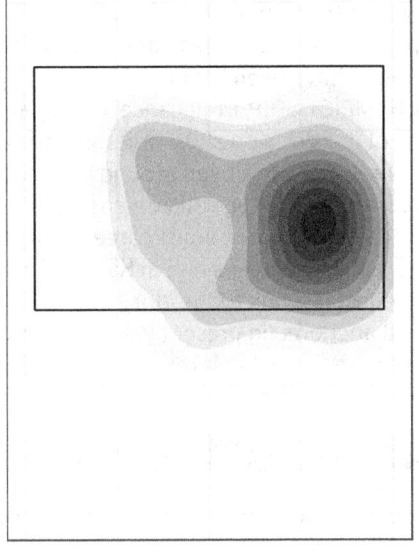

Brett Phillips OF

Born: 05/30/94 Age: 25 Bats: L Throws: R
Height: 6'0" Weight: 185 Origin: Round 6, 2012 Draft (#189 overall)

YEAR	TEAM	LVL	AGE	PA	R	2B	3B	HR	RBI	BB	K	SB	CS	AVG/OBP/SLG
2016	BLX	AA	22	517	60	14	6	16	62	67	154	12	7	.229/.332/.397
2017	CSP	AAA	23	432	79	23	10	19	78	45	129	9	1	.305/.377/.567
2017	MIL	MLB	23	98	9	3	0	4	12	9	34	5	0	.276/.351/.448
2018	CSP	AAA	24	299	42	12	7	6	25	36	94	11	0	.240/.331/.411
2018	MIL	MLB	24	24	2	0	1	0	4	2	11	0	0	.182/.250/.273
2018	KCA	MLB	24	123	13	4	2	2	7	9	50	1	1	.188/.252/.313
2019	KCA	MLB	25	361	42	13	4	12	40	34	120	6	1	.215/.292/.393

Breakout: 8% Improve: 30% Collapse: 7% Attrition: 24% MLB: 51%
Comparables: Brent Clevlen, Rymer Liriano, Matt Joyce

Here are two truths and a lie about Phillips, acquired by the Royals in the trade-deadline deal that sent Mike Moustakas to the Cream City. 1: He struck out in more than 40 percent of his major-league plate appearances in 2018. 2: His right arm is the stuff of legend, a missile launcher that leaves baserunners vaporized in the shape of their former bodies before they dissolve in a heap of smoldering ash, Wile E. Coyote-style. 3: He has a very soft, gentle, unassuming laugh. Answer: #3 is the lie. His laugh can range from piercing pterodactyl's screech to a guttural donkey's bray, stretching his face into a rictus so taut that one's own cheek muscles twinge in sympathetic pain. But as YouTube commenter "Wawa 123" noted about a video of said laugh, "Lol This guy is going to be known more for his laugh than his baseball abilities." Whether #1 improves will determine if major-league fans will get to enjoy #2 and #3. Laugh, and the world laughs with you; strike out, and you walk back to the dugout alone.

YEAR	TEAM	LVL	AGE	PA	DRC+	VORP	BABIP	BRR	FRAA	WARP
2016	BLX	AA	22	517	101	24.9	.311	1.5	CF(102): 0.8, RF(19): 0.0	0.8
2017	CSP	AAA	23	432	128	30.5	.412	2.1	RF(52): -3.2, CF(49): 3.9	2.4
2017	MIL	MLB	23	98	90	6.6	.408	0.3	CF(26): 4.8, RF(9): -0.3	0.7
2018	CSP	AAA	24	299	76	10.7	.346	1.1	RF(34): 2.9, CF(20): -1.8	-0.2
2018	MIL	MLB	24	24	43	-1.0	.364	0.0	RF(7): -0.6, CF(5): 0.5	-0.1
2018	KCA	MLB	24	123	46	-1.8	.311	0.3	CF(23): 4.4, RF(9): 0.3	0.1
2019	KCA	MLB	25	361	85	5.3	.298	1.0	RF 1, CF 0	0.6

Brett Phillips, continued

Batted Ball Distribution

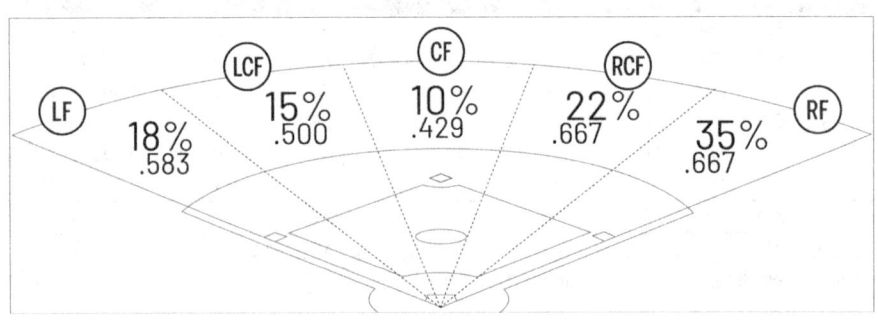

Strike Zone vs LHP   Strike Zone vs RHP

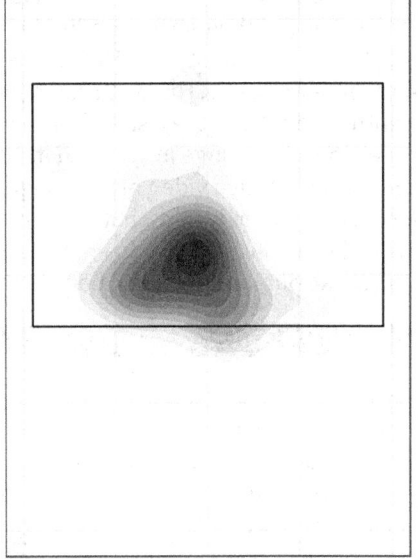

Jorge Soler   RF

Born: 02/25/92   Age: 27   Bats: R   Throws: R
Height: 6'4"   Weight: 230   Origin: International Free Agent, 2012

YEAR	TEAM	LVL	AGE	PA	R	2B	3B	HR	RBI	BB	K	SB	CS	AVG/OBP/SLG
2016	TEN	AA	24	42	4	0	0	0	2	11	11	0	0	.167/.381/.167
2016	CHN	MLB	24	264	37	9	0	12	31	31	66	0	0	.238/.333/.436
2017	OMA	AAA	25	327	49	9	0	24	59	50	82	1	0	.267/.388/.564
2017	KCA	MLB	25	110	7	5	0	2	6	12	36	0	0	.144/.245/.258
2018	KCA	MLB	26	257	27	18	0	9	28	28	69	3	1	.265/.354/.466
2019	KCA	MLB	27	508	60	19	2	19	64	57	132	2	1	.233/.325/.413

Breakout: 7%   Improve: 56%   Collapse: 13%   Attrition: 13%   MLB: 93%
Comparables: Kyle Blanks, Shin-Soo Choo, Matt Joyce

The wave of Cuban emigres into the major leagues over the past decade has tended to bifurcate pretty sharply along the curves of success and failure. Among the higher-profile signings, Yoenis Cespedes, Jose Abreu, Yasiel Puig, and Yuli Gurriel are the success stories. Yasmany Tomas, Rusney Castillo, Alex Guerrero, and Hector Olivera (you forgot about him, didn't you?) have to be counted as the opposite. Soler appeared to fall into the latter after two disappointing seasons with the Cubs and a trade to the Royals that led to nearly a full year of "meh" in the offense-friendly PCL in 2017. Cue 2018, when Soler began the season in Kansas City, doing a plausible impression of "middle-of-the-order bat." A broken big toe truncated his season in late May, leaving us to wonder if a small, productive sample portends anything bigger. He should be fully recovered by spring training and will try to make a case to be counted among the happier stories of recent Cuban imports.

YEAR	TEAM	LVL	AGE	PA	DRC+	VORP	BABIP	BRR	FRAA	WARP
2016	TEN	AA	24	42	108	0.1	.250	0.0	LF(6): -0.5	0.0
2016	CHN	MLB	24	264	99	13.9	.276	-0.4	LF(53): -2.7, RF(7): -1.1	0.2
2017	OMA	AAA	25	327	147	25.8	.293	-2.0	RF(39): -0.4, LF(23): 3.0	2.1
2017	KCA	MLB	25	110	64	-8.6	.203	-0.3	RF(15): -1.6, LF(7): 0.8	-0.4
2018	KCA	MLB	26	257	101	11.9	.340	-0.5	RF(52): -1.0	0.4
2019	KCA	MLB	27	508	101	9.0	.281	-0.6	RF 0	1.0

Jorge Soler, continued

Batted Ball Distribution

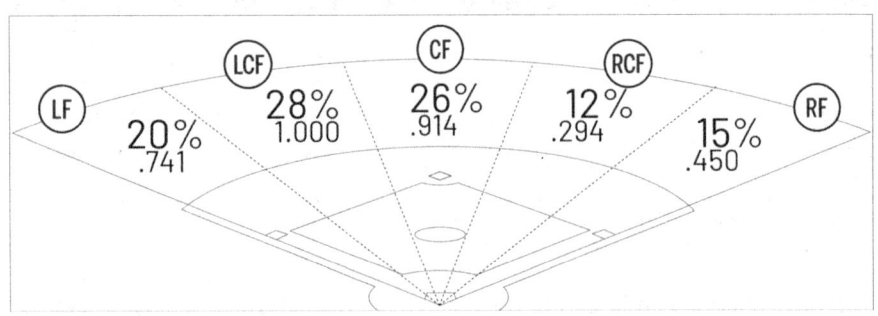

Strike Zone vs LHP   **Strike Zone vs RHP**

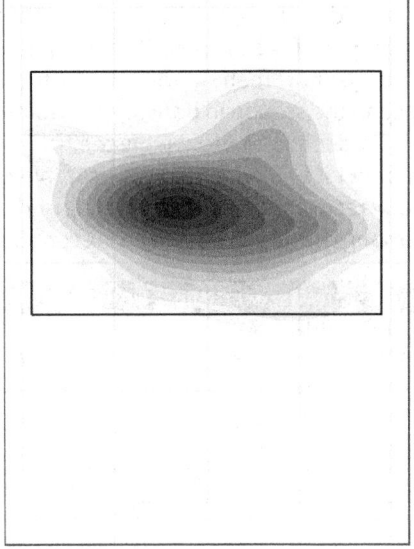

Jason Adam   RHP

Born: 08/04/91   Age: 27   Bats: R   Throws: R
Height: 6'4"   Weight: 225   Origin: Round 5, 2010 Draft (#149 overall)

YEAR	TEAM	LVL	AGE	W	L	SV	G	GS	IP	H	HR	BB/9	K/9	K	GB%	BABIP
2017	NWA	AA	25	0	0	0	5	0	6^1	3	0	5.7	15.6	11	27%	.273
2018	NWA	AA	26	1	0	0	6	0	11^1	5	0	3.2	13.5	17	36%	.227
2018	KCA	MLB	26	0	3	0	31	0	32^1	30	9	4.2	10.3	37	29%	.269
2018	OMA	AAA	26	2	0	4	11	0	12^2	6	0	5.0	10.7	15	34%	.207
2019	KCA	MLB	27	2	1	1	37	0	39^2	37	6	5.0	10.2	45	36%	.307

Breakout: 20%   Improve: 39%   Collapse: 8%   Attrition: 20%   MLB: 56%
Comparables: Francisco Rosario, Scott Mathieson, Gonzalez Germen

For most of a three-month stretch last summer, Adam was a useful righty bullpen arm, even if that arm was deployed in low-leverage situations (to be fair, the 2018 Royals rarely had any other type of leverage). On August 17, facing the White Sox, he surrendered five earned runs on two homers, two singles, and a walk. His ERA shot up from 4.78 to 6.12, where it will forever live on his 2018 stat line, as Adam was sent down to Omaha the next day never to return, even to an expanded September roster. (Oh, the statistical tragedy of small samples for fringy relief arms.) Dependent on a fastball-curve combo that yields both strikeouts and home runs in abundance, Adams should be once again in the mix for a bullpen role and have a chance to keep that unfortunate 2018 line from being the last one on the back of his baseball card.

YEAR	TEAM	LVL	AGE	WHIP	ERA	DRA	WARP	MPH	FB%	WHF	CSP
2017	NWA	AA	25	1.11	7.11	2.58	0.2				
2018	NWA	AA	26	0.79	1.59	3.89	0.1				
2018	KCA	MLB	26	1.39	6.12	7.04	-0.8	96.0	61.1	13.1	45.6
2018	OMA	AAA	26	1.03	1.42	2.80	0.3				
2019	KCA	MLB	27	1.50	4.85	5.07	0.0	95.5	61.9	13.3	46.2

Jason Adam, continued

Pitch Shape vs LHH

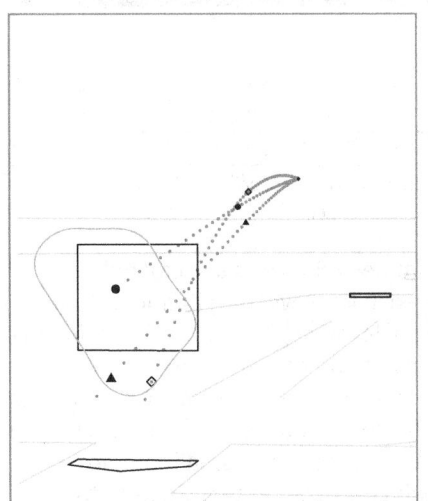

Pitch Shape vs RHH

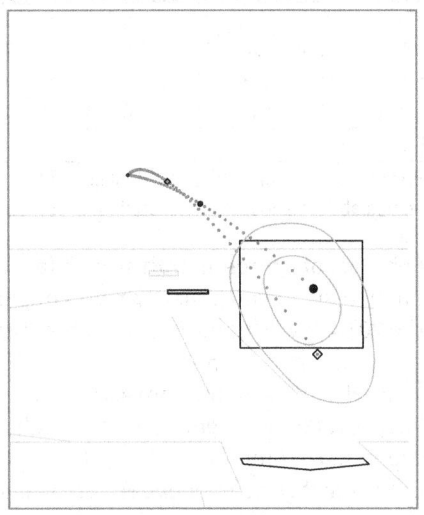

Type	Frequency	Velocity	H Movement	V Movement
● Fastball	61.1%	94.5 [107]	-6.1 [103]	-13 [109]
□ Sinker				
+ Cutter				
▲ Changeup	7.9%	89.5 [117]	-12.8 [92]	-26.5 [102]
× Splitter				
▽ Slider				
◇ Curveball	31.0%	77.8 [98]	13.4 [123]	-48.2 [100]
⊕ Slow Curveball				
✳ Knuckleball				
▼ Screwball				

Homer Bailey RHP

Born: 05/03/86 Age: 33 Bats: R Throws: R
Height: 6'4" Weight: 223 Origin: Round 1, 2004 Draft (#7 overall)

YEAR	TEAM	LVL	AGE	W	L	SV	G	GS	IP	H	HR	BB/9	K/9	K	GB%	BABIP
2016	LOU	AAA	30	1	2	0	7	7	24	31	7	3.4	7.1	19	54%	.312
2016	CIN	MLB	30	2	3	0	6	6	23	35	2	2.7	10.6	27	47%	.452
2017	CIN	MLB	31	6	9	0	18	18	91	112	11	4.2	6.6	67	46%	.346
2018	LOU	AAA	32	2	2	0	7	6	37²	41	4	2.4	6.7	28	37%	.311
2018	CIN	MLB	32	1	14	0	20	20	106¹	141	23	2.8	6.3	75	44%	.327
2019	KCA	MLB	33	5	9	0	22	22	110¹	133	18	3.6	6.5	80	44%	.322

Breakout: 14%   Improve: 32%   Collapse: 20%   Attrition: 13%   MLB: 71%
Comparables: Jerome Williams, Jeff Francis, Matt Cain

If Bailey had reached free agency this year instead of next, his agent would take pains to show that the big Texan's arm was finally healthy, he reached the 100-inning plateau for the first time in ages and improved his ERA for the third straight season. That's why you should never listen to an agent talking about his player. Bailey missed two months with a sore knee but his arm was sound, making his horror show of a season all the more disappointing. He allowed a league-worst .901 OPS. Batters in the eight-hole hit .390/.490/.585 against him (the MLB average is .233/.302/370). The Reds lost 19 of the 20 games he started before mercifully pulling the plug in early September. The calls are coming from inside the house. One year. $28 million. Breathe deep. All but the major-league minimum will be picked up by the Dodgers, who immediately released him upon his trade from Cincinnati

YEAR	TEAM	LVL	AGE	WHIP	ERA	DRA	WARP	MPH	FB%	WHF	CSP
2016	LOU	AAA	30	1.67	5.62	4.52	0.2				
2016	CIN	MLB	30	1.83	6.65	3.82	0.4	96.0	54.2	9.8	44.6
2017	CIN	MLB	31	1.69	6.43	7.38	-1.8	95.4	57	10.2	48
2018	LOU	AAA	32	1.35	4.78	4.03	0.6				
2018	CIN	MLB	32	1.64	6.09	6.03	-0.9	95.2	56	9.8	49.6
2019	KCA	MLB	33	1.61	5.37	5.65	-0.2	94.3	55.5	9.8	47.2

Homer Bailey, continued

Pitch Shape vs LHH

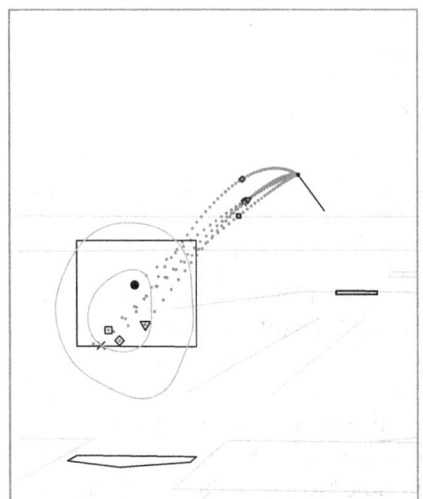

Pitch Shape vs RHH

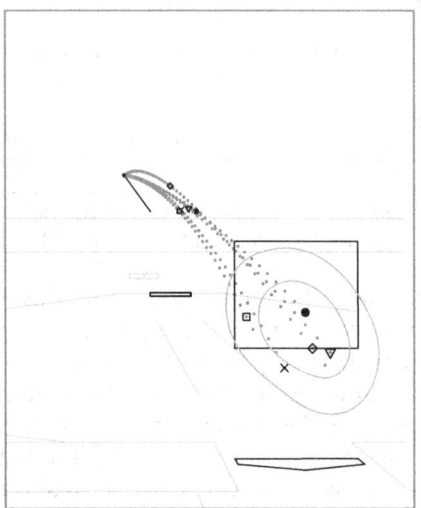

Type	Frequency	Velocity	H Movement	V Movement
● Fastball	44.4%	93.8 [104]	-6.9 [99]	-15.3 [101]
☐ Sinker	11.6%	93.4 [105]	-12.3 [103]	-17.9 [108]
+ Cutter	1.4%	90.1 [108]	1.1 [96]	-23 [103]
▲ Changeup	0.9%	87.1 [107]	-11.4 [100]	-24.1 [110]
✕ Splitter	14.5%	86.2 [103]	-8.5 [99]	-27.8 [107]
▽ Slider	17.4%	87.9 [115]	2.2 [89]	-26.5 [119]
◇ Curveball	9.8%	79.9 [105]	8.8 [104]	-45.7 [105]
⊕ Slow Curveball				
✳ Knuckleball				
▼ Screwball				

Scott Barlow   RHP

Born: 12/18/92   Age: 26   Bats: R   Throws: R
Height: 6'3"   Weight: 215   Origin: Round 6, 2011 Draft (#194 overall)

YEAR	TEAM	LVL	AGE	W	L	SV	G	GS	IP	H	HR	BB/9	K/9	K	GB%	BABIP
2016	TUL	AA	23	4	7	0	24	23	124^1	125	9	3.8	7.4	102	45%	.306
2017	OKL	AAA	24	1	3	0	7	7	32^1	37	6	6.4	10.0	36	37%	.333
2017	TUL	AA	24	6	3	0	19	19	107^1	60	9	3.1	10.4	124	45%	.211
2018	KCA	MLB	25	1	1	0	6	0	15	16	2	1.8	9.0	15	40%	.311
2018	OMA	AAA	25	1	4	1	13	10	45^2	54	9	4.1	9.9	50	38%	.357
2019	KCA	MLB	26	3	4	0	34	8	67	65	9	4.1	8.5	64	40%	.294

Breakout: 7%   Improve: 23%   Collapse: 10%   Attrition: 21%   MLB: 44%
Comparables: Jeff Niemann, Tyler Anderson, Chris Stratton

At this point, the Royals would be happy to have a player who ranks at the top of *any* list not beginning with "Most Disappointing..." or "Whatever Happened To..." As it happens, in former Dodger farmhand Barlow, they currently have 2017's #1 ranked minor-league free agent, according to Chris Mitchell's stat-line-scouting KATOH system. That might seem like damnation by faint praise, and it assuredly is, but the baseball intelligentsia loves these types (Wilmer Font and Willians Astudillo were on last year's list), so if you're looking for a player upon which to plant your hipster flag, Barlow is a deep-ballot candidate. The righty doesn't wow with raw stuff—hence the "minor-league free agent" part—but he acquitted himself well in his brief time in Kansas City and may have a chance to go mainstream in 2019.

YEAR	TEAM	LVL	AGE	WHIP	ERA	DRA	WARP	MPH	FB%	WHF	CSP
2016	TUL	AA	23	1.42	3.98	3.40	2.5				
2017	OKL	AAA	24	1.86	7.24	4.48	0.4				
2017	TUL	AA	24	0.90	2.10	3.33	2.4				
2018	KCA	MLB	25	1.27	3.60	3.69	0.2	93.1	53	11.9	50.8
2018	OMA	AAA	25	1.64	6.11	3.71	0.9				
2019	KCA	MLB	26	1.42	4.49	4.83	0.4	92.7	53.9	12.1	51.7

Scott Barlow, continued

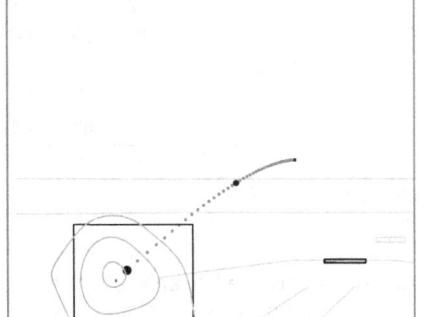
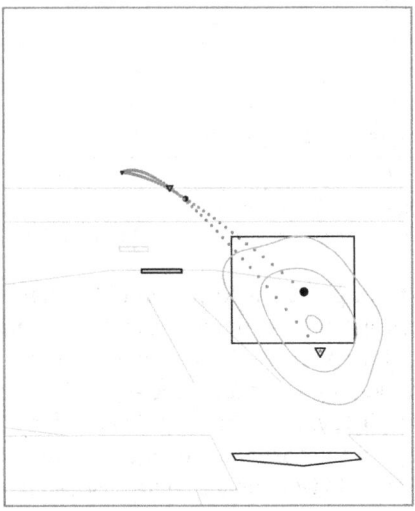

Type	Frequency	Velocity	H Movement	V Movement
● Fastball	53.0%	91.2 [96]	0.1 [131]	-17.3 [95]
□ Sinker				
+ Cutter				
▲ Changeup	5.5%	86.4 [104]	-13.1 [90]	-24.9 [107]
× Splitter				
▽ Slider	26.7%	80.7 [83]	9.6 [120]	-39.9 [80]
◇ Curveball	14.8%	75.8 [90]	13 [122]	-53.3 [88]
⊕ Slow Curveball				
✳ Knuckleball				
▼ Screwball				

Brad Boxberger RHP

Born: 05/27/88 Age: 31 Bats: R Throws: R
Height: 6'2" Weight: 205 Origin: Round 1, 2009 Draft (#43 overall)

YEAR	TEAM	LVL	AGE	W	L	SV	G	GS	IP	H	HR	BB/9	K/9	K	GB%	BABIP
2016	TBA	MLB	28	4	3	0	27	0	24^1	23	3	7.0	8.1	22	49%	.294
2017	TBA	MLB	29	4	4	0	30	0	29^1	23	4	3.4	12.3	40	46%	.292
2018	ARI	MLB	30	3	7	32	60	0	53^1	44	9	5.4	12.0	71	48%	.287
2019	KCA	MLB	31	3	3	11	52	0	54^2	47	5	5.0	9.8	59	45%	.294

Breakout: 22% Improve: 35% Collapse: 28% Attrition: 15% MLB: 88%
Comparables: Boone Logan, Sergio Santos, Mike Dunn

Balling on a budget is great, but it's also important to remember you usually get what you pay for. Arizona has done plenty of bargain hunting in acquiring closers over the last five years. The Addison Reed experiment didn't really work. Brad Ziegler was reliable if not remarkable. Daniel Hudson got a few chances and then the Fernando Rodney Experience came to town. Digging into the depths yet again yielded Boxberger for 2018, and for a pitcher whose stuff is pretty meh, the results were pretty good ... for a while. Then reality set in and things took a steep dive, both on the mound and in the win column. He struck out plenty of hitters despite mediocre whiff rates, but walked more than his share and paid the price. His days as a closer may very well be over for good.

YEAR	TEAM	LVL	AGE	WHIP	ERA	DRA	WARP	MPH	FB%	WHF	CSP
2016	TBA	MLB	28	1.73	4.81	6.17	-0.3	94.5	59.2	11.5	46.4
2017	TBA	MLB	29	1.16	3.38	2.89	0.7	94.2	65.6	14.3	49.4
2018	ARI	MLB	30	1.42	4.39	5.11	-0.1	93.4	66.3	11.5	46.7
2019	KCA	MLB	31	1.41	3.88	4.25	0.6	92.9	64.5	12.1	47.3

Kansas City Royals 2019

Brad Boxberger, continued

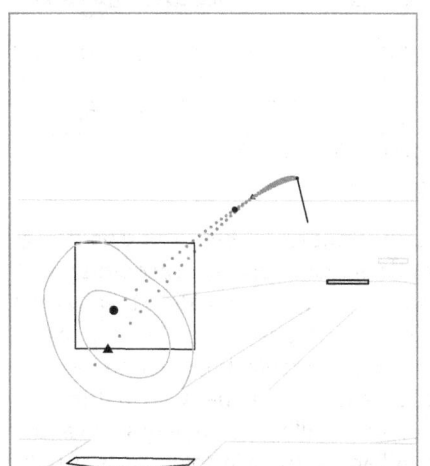
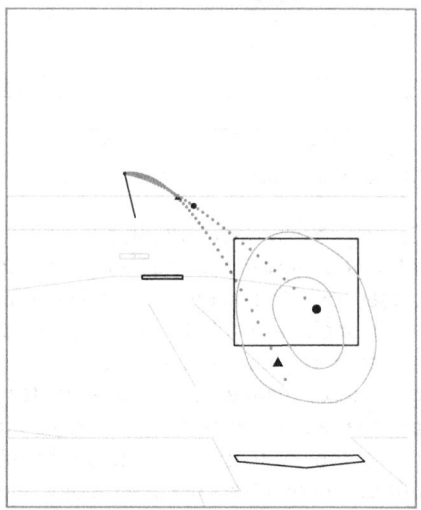

Type	Frequency	Velocity	H Movement	V Movement
● Fastball	66.3%	91.7 [98]	-2.7 [118]	-16.6 [97]
☐ Sinker				
+ Cutter				
▲ Changeup	30.7%	80.1 [79]	-11.5 [99]	-34.6 [79]
✕ Splitter				
▽ Slider	3.1%	86.1 [107]	6.5 [107]	-28.6 [113]
◇ Curveball				
⊕ Slow Curveball				
✻ Knuckleball				
▼ Screwball				

Jake Diekman   LHP

Born: 01/21/87   Age: 32   Bats: L   Throws: L
Height: 6'4"   Weight: 200   Origin: Round 30, 2007 Draft (#923 overall)

YEAR	TEAM	LVL	AGE	W	L	SV	G	GS	IP	H	HR	BB/9	K/9	K	GB%	BABIP
2016	TEX	MLB	29	4	2	4	66	0	53	36	4	4.4	10.0	59	50%	.248
2017	TEX	MLB	30	0	0	1	11	0	10^2	4	1	8.4	11.0	13	59%	.143
2018	TEX	MLB	31	1	1	2	47	0	39	31	2	5.3	11.1	48	48%	.302
2018	ARI	MLB	31	0	1	0	24	0	14^1	18	2	5.0	11.3	18	57%	.400
2019	KCA	MLB	32	3	3	0	52	0	54^2	49	5	4.9	9.6	59	48%	.298

Breakout: 22%   Improve: 41%   Collapse: 21%   Attrition: 9%   MLB: 86%
Comparables: Adam Ottavino, Fernando Rodney, Jim Kern

Strikeouts are good. Walks are bad. With Diekman, you get plenty of each. The Diamondbacks acquired him from the Rangers at the deadline, hoping to shore up a weakness in the bullpen against lefty swingers. Instead, they got a guy who weirdly struggled against same-handed hitters, including too many walks and some untimely long balls — just in time for the team's epic September collapse. Diekman has always walked a fine line between being dominant and disastrous, and his time in the desert was too much of the latter. On the right contract, he's a useful bullpen piece, but don't get your hopes up. He'll dash them quicker than he can issue four balls.

YEAR	TEAM	LVL	AGE	WHIP	ERA	DRA	WARP	MPH	FB%	WHF	CSP
2016	TEX	MLB	29	1.17	3.40	4.73	0.1	97.7	73.6	12.1	42.1
2017	TEX	MLB	30	1.31	2.53	7.02	-0.2	97.5	68.1	12.2	37.4
2018	TEX	MLB	31	1.38	3.69	6.34	-0.6	96.8	62.4	11.4	45.4
2018	ARI	MLB	31	1.81	7.53	6.25	-0.2	97.2	67.9	13.5	46.8
2019	KCA	MLB	32	1.44	3.98	4.34	0.5	96.3	66.8	11.9	41.7

Jake Diekman, continued

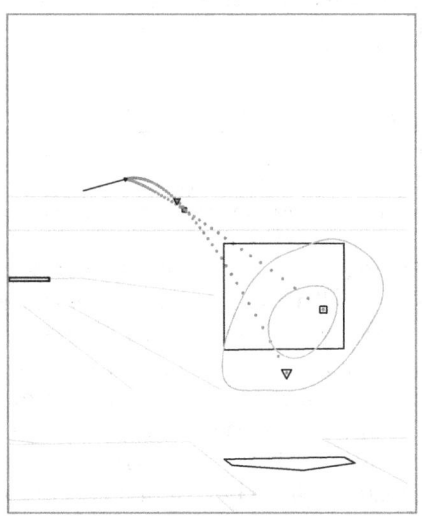

Type	Frequency	Velocity	H Movement	V Movement
● Fastball				
□ Sinker	63.9%	95.4 [115]	13.4 [93]	-17.5 [109]
+ Cutter				
▲ Changeup				
× Splitter				
▽ Slider	36.1%	83.3 [95]	-5.6 [103]	-38.3 [84]
◇ Curveball				
⊕ Slow Curveball				
✳ Knuckleball				
▼ Screwball				

Danny Duffy LHP

Born: 12/21/88 Age: 30 Bats: L Throws: L
Height: 6'3" Weight: 205 Origin: Round 3, 2007 Draft (#96 overall)

YEAR	TEAM	LVL	AGE	W	L	SV	G	GS	IP	H	HR	BB/9	K/9	K	GB%	BABIP
2016	KCA	MLB	27	12	3	0	42	26	179^2	163	27	2.1	9.4	188	37%	.291
2017	KCA	MLB	28	9	10	0	24	24	146^1	143	13	2.5	8.0	130	41%	.309
2018	KCA	MLB	29	8	12	0	28	28	155	161	23	4.1	8.2	141	36%	.304
2019	KCA	MLB	30	8	11	0	28	28	159	159	23	3.1	7.8	137	38%	.291

Breakout: 6% Improve: 34% Collapse: 36% Attrition: 11% MLB: 94%
Comparables: Yovani Gallardo, Jason Hammel, Gavin Floyd

Duffy would rather you not read these projections. The Royals' ace, struggling through his most trying season since his rookie year, has long been critical of baseball analytics and its inability to measure the heart within a person: their camaraderie, their mood, their focus. In one sense, he's correct: all projection systems inculcate a sense of over-certainty. That one line there looks like what he's supposed to do in 2019, but it's really only the most likely result, a plurality, barely more possible than any other. In another sense, though, he's also right, because PECOTA not only fails to see into Duffy's heart, it also can't investigate his left arm. He underwent elbow surgery after the end of 2017 and one could make the case, though again without certainty, that he simply never got right afterward, finally culminating in a September shutdown. While the pure numbers on his stuff looked fine, Duffy struggled badly to keep his breaking pitches down, leading to extra baserunners and extra home runs with baserunners on. We can make our best guess on his performance–really, it's our job–but when 2019 arrives and Duffy readies himself for a new season, we'll all find out together.

YEAR	TEAM	LVL	AGE	WHIP	ERA	DRA	WARP	MPH	FB%	WHF	CSP
2016	KCA	MLB	27	1.14	3.51	3.65	3.5	97.8	59.4	14	49.4
2017	KCA	MLB	28	1.26	3.81	3.87	2.8	94.8	47.3	12.3	50.6
2018	KCA	MLB	29	1.49	4.88	5.54	-0.4	95.5	55.7	10.8	49.6
2019	KCA	MLB	30	1.34	4.41	4.84	1.1	95.2	54.1	12	49.7

Danny Duffy, continued

Pitch Shape vs LHH

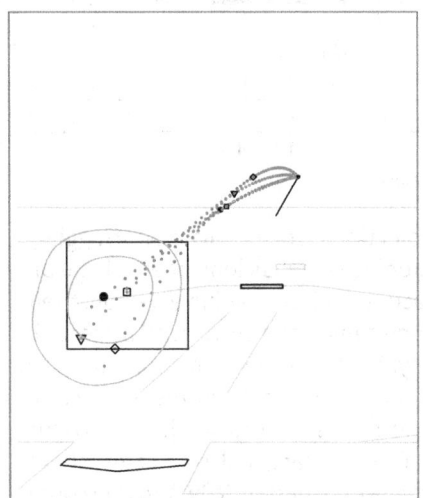

Pitch Shape vs RHH

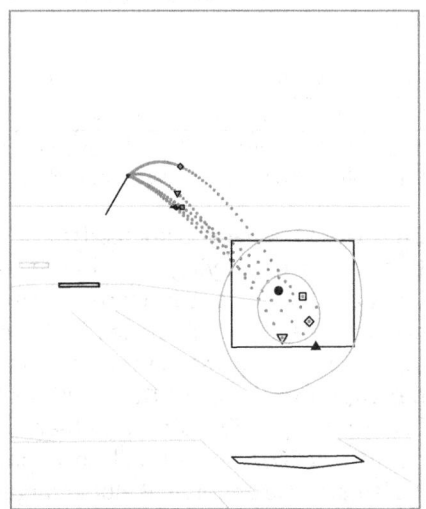

Type	Frequency	Velocity	H Movement	V Movement
● Fastball	43.6%	93.7 [104]	7.1 [98]	-12 [112]
□ Sinker	12.1%	93.5 [105]	10.9 [114]	-14.2 [120]
+ Cutter				
▲ Changeup	18.6%	84.2 [95]	13.8 [87]	-24.1 [109]
× Splitter				
▽ Slider	16.2%	83.9 [97]	-3.6 [95]	-35.9 [92]
◇ Curveball	9.5%	76.5 [93]	-6.6 [95]	-55.4 [83]
⊕ Slow Curveball				
✳ Knuckleball				
▼ Screwball				

Heath Fillmyer RHP

Born: 05/16/94 Age: 25 Bats: R Throws: R
Height: 6'1" Weight: 195 Origin: Round 5, 2014 Draft (#162 overall)

YEAR	TEAM	LVL	AGE	W	L	SV	G	GS	IP	H	HR	BB/9	K/9	K	GB%	BABIP
2016	STO	A+	22	5	6	0	18	16	95	101	4	2.9	8.4	89	44%	.328
2016	MID	AA	22	2	0	0	8	8	39	31	3	1.8	6.7	29	47%	.259
2017	MID	AA	23	11	5	0	29	29	149^2	158	19	3.1	6.9	115	45%	.310
2018	OMA	AAA	24	4	5	0	13	13	67^1	82	5	3.7	6.3	47	44%	.342
2018	KCA	MLB	24	4	2	0	17	13	82^1	78	11	3.5	6.2	57	46%	.277
2019	KCA	MLB	25	3	4	0	29	8	61	65	9	3.6	6.8	47	43%	.296

Breakout: 26% Improve: 36% Collapse: 22% Attrition: 41% MLB: 70%
Comparables: T.J. McFarland, Allen Webster, Cody Anderson

In the spring of 2018, radio station "New Jersey 101.5" ran a piece on their website: "Major League via Jersey: 2018 MLB Players Born in NJ." No surprises at the top: Trout, of course, then Todd Frazier, Rick Porcello, Brad Brach, and so on. Fillmyer, of Roebling, just across the Delaware River from Levittown, Pennsylvania, had not yet made his major-league debut and was thus not eligible for this list. Ranking him among the similarly fringy arms in the Royals system isn't much fun, but where would he fit on the New Jersey list after a competent-but-forgettable debut season? A quick eyeballing suggests right around #11, nestled just below fifth-outfielder Matt Szczur and Orioles hurler Jimmy Yacabonis (and if you think that ranking was determined by a desire to type the name "Jimmy Yacabonis" in this comment, you are correct). Fillmyer's fastball-slider profile may not be good enough to bring glory to the Garden State, but neither will he bring it shame.

YEAR	TEAM	LVL	AGE	WHIP	ERA	DRA	WARP	MPH	FB%	WHF	CSP
2016	STO	A+	22	1.39	3.60	4.03	1.5				
2016	MID	AA	22	1.00	2.54	3.89	0.6				
2017	MID	AA	23	1.40	3.49	3.77	2.5				
2018	OMA	AAA	24	1.63	5.75	4.19	1.0				
2018	KCA	MLB	24	1.34	4.26	5.47	-0.2	94.3	52.5	9.7	45.8
2019	KCA	MLB	25	1.46	4.95	5.25	0.0	94.0	53.7	10	46.9

Heath Fillmyer, continued

Pitch Shape vs LHH   Pitch Shape vs RHH

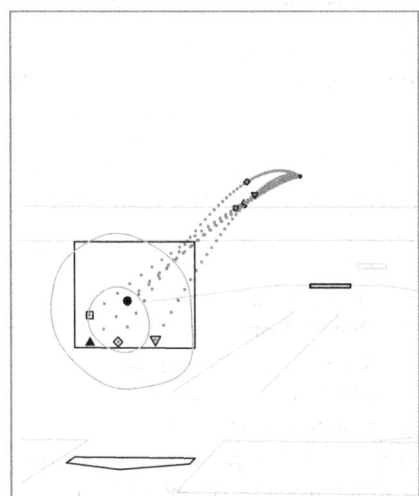 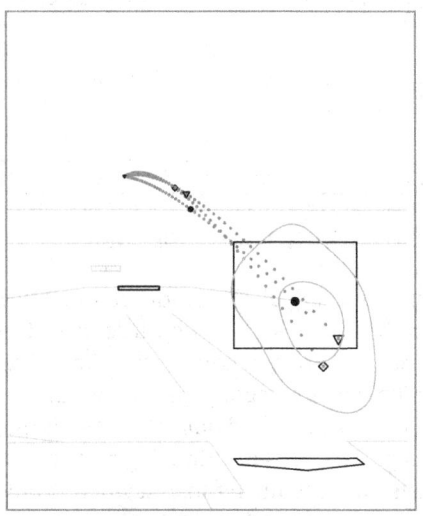

Type	Frequency	Velocity	H Movement	V Movement
● Fastball	48.2%	92.9 [101]	-4.3 [111]	-15.2 [102]
□ Sinker	4.2%	92.3 [99]	-11.1 [112]	-18.3 [107]
+ Cutter				
▲ Changeup	14.7%	85.8 [102]	-11.7 [98]	-28.9 [95]
× Splitter				
▽ Slider	22.4%	84.4 [100]	2.3 [89]	-34.4 [96]
◇ Curveball	10.4%	79.7 [105]	3.8 [83]	-44.9 [107]
✥ Slow Curveball				
✳ Knuckleball				
▼ Screwball				

Brian Flynn LHP

Born: 04/19/90 Age: 29 Bats: L Throws: L
Height: 6'7" Weight: 255 Origin: Round 7, 2011 Draft (#227 overall)

YEAR	TEAM	LVL	AGE	W	L	SV	G	GS	IP	H	HR	BB/9	K/9	K	GB%	BABIP
2016	OMA	AAA	26	2	1	0	9	4	23^2	22	1	4.6	10.6	28	66%	.350
2016	KCA	MLB	26	1	2	0	36	1	55^1	38	5	3.7	7.2	44	57%	.223
2017	OMA	AAA	27	5	3	0	22	4	50	68	10	2.2	9.0	50	46%	.369
2017	KCA	MLB	27	0	0	0	1	0	2^1	3	0	0.0	0.0	0	38%	.375
2018	KCA	MLB	28	3	5	1	48	0	75^2	87	5	4.2	5.6	47	51%	.333
2019	KCA	MLB	29	3	3	0	57	0	60	63	8	4.1	7.0	47	49%	.303

Breakout: 29% Improve: 37% Collapse: 26% Attrition: 26% MLB: 70%
Comparables: Vin Mazzaro, Jared Hughes, Alex Wilson

If you Google "Brian Flynn serviceable reliever," you'll find roughly one page worth of hits, enough to suggest that Flynn has self-actualized to a rare and impressive degree. A groundballer with average velocity and average baseball facial hair who doesn't strike many folks out, the imposing 6'7" lefty logged the most relief innings for the Royals in 2018. Entering his first year of arbitration, he may be back for another 75 innings next year—not that you'd notice.

YEAR	TEAM	LVL	AGE	WHIP	ERA	DRA	WARP	MPH	FB%	WHF	CSP
2016	OMA	AAA	26	1.44	3.04	3.36	0.5				
2016	KCA	MLB	26	1.10	2.60	4.41	0.4	95.4	66.7	11.6	42
2017	OMA	AAA	27	1.60	5.40	2.82	1.4				
2017	KCA	MLB	27	1.29	3.86	7.08	0.0	94.2	65.5	0	58.1
2018	KCA	MLB	28	1.61	4.04	6.59	-1.5	94.0	68.7	8.9	46.7
2019	KCA	MLB	29	1.53	5.07	5.20	0.0	93.8	68.1	9.5	49.3

Kansas City Royals 2019

Brian Flynn, continued

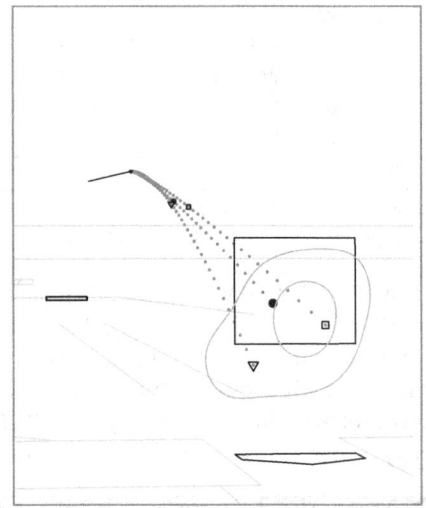

Pitch Shape vs LHH / Pitch Shape vs RHH

Type	Frequency	Velocity	H Movement	V Movement
● Fastball	21.5%	92.7 [101]	6.8 [100]	-16.6 [97]
☐ Sinker	47.2%	92.1 [98]	11.8 [107]	-20.2 [100]
+ Cutter				
▲ Changeup	0.6%	84 [95]	12.8 [92]	-28.3 [97]
✕ Splitter				
▽ Slider	30.7%	86 [107]	-2.6 [90]	-31 [106]
◇ Curveball	0.1%	80.6 [108]	-3.8 [83]	-40.8 [116]
⊕ Slow Curveball				
✳ Knuckleball				
▼ Screwball				

66 - Royals Player Analysis

Jake Junis   RHP

Born: 09/16/92   Age: 26   Bats: R   Throws: R
Height: 6'2"   Weight: 225   Origin: Round 29, 2011 Draft (#876 overall)

YEAR	TEAM	LVL	AGE	W	L	SV	G	GS	IP	H	HR	BB/9	K/9	K	GB%	BABIP
2016	NWA	AA	23	9	7	0	21	21	119	110	12	2.0	8.8	117	43%	.302
2016	OMA	AAA	23	1	3	0	6	6	30	39	6	2.1	7.8	26	41%	.367
2017	OMA	AAA	24	3	5	0	12	12	71	61	6	1.9	10.9	86	37%	.307
2017	KCA	MLB	24	9	3	0	20	16	98[1]	101	15	2.3	7.3	80	42%	.294
2018	KCA	MLB	25	9	12	0	30	30	177	182	32	2.2	8.3	164	43%	.298
2019	KCA	MLB	26	9	10	0	28	28	159	160	21	2.6	7.9	141	41%	.297

Breakout: 29%   Improve: 44%   Collapse: 19%   Attrition: 20%   MLB: 86%
Comparables: Matt Boyd, Taylor Buchholz, Justin Grimm

Over the course of the season, Junis logged 177 innings, making him the de facto workhorse of a beleaguered staff. And while the limited light of national attention on the Royals shone on the breakout of Adalberto Mondesi, the second half of 2018 saw a step forward from Junis that may have gotten lost in the shadows. Struggling with control in the middle of the season, Junis heeded the advice of pitching coach Cal Eldred to get back to basics, throwing his four-seam fastball more often. The result: He dramatically cut both walks and home runs—but it remains to be seen if a fastball-slider combo is enough for Junis to thrive as a starter. On a rebuilding team, he'll certainly get every chance to prove it.

YEAR	TEAM	LVL	AGE	WHIP	ERA	DRA	WARP	MPH	FB%	WHF	CSP
2016	NWA	AA	23	1.15	3.25	3.21	2.7				
2016	OMA	AAA	23	1.53	7.20	4.84	0.2				
2017	OMA	AAA	24	1.07	2.92	3.16	2.0				
2017	KCA	MLB	24	1.28	4.30	4.88	0.7	93.1	55.3	9.9	51.8
2018	KCA	MLB	25	1.27	4.37	5.53	-0.4	93.0	53.3	10.3	49.2
2019	KCA	MLB	26	1.30	4.12	4.53	1.6	92.7	54.9	10.4	51.2

Kansas City Royals 2019

Jake Junis, continued

Pitch Shape vs LHH

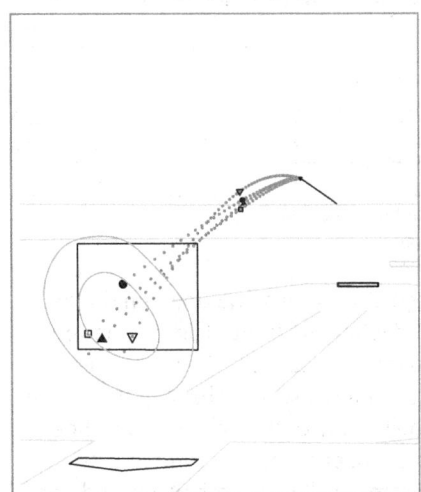

Pitch Shape vs RHH

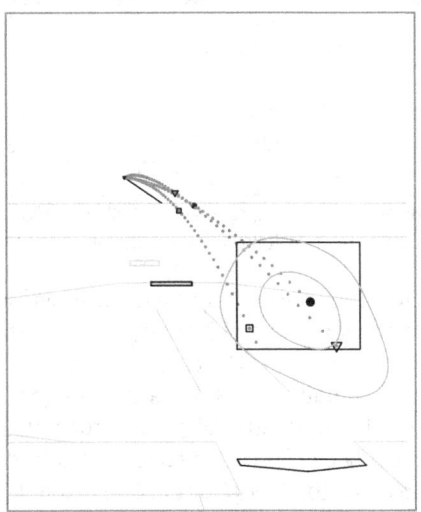

Type	Frequency	Velocity	H Movement	V Movement
● Fastball	33.3%	91.8 [98]	-5.3 [106]	-17 [96]
□ Sinker	20.1%	91.1 [93]	-12.6 [100]	-22.4 [93]
+ Cutter				
▲ Changeup	5.9%	85.2 [100]	-7.5 [120]	-28.9 [95]
× Splitter				
▽ Slider	40.1%	82.2 [90]	13 [135]	-38.6 [84]
◇ Curveball	0.7%	80.2 [107]	12.5 [120]	-43.7 [110]
⊕ Slow Curveball				
✶ Knuckleball				
▼ Screwball				

Brad Keller RHP

Born: 07/27/95 Age: 23 Bats: R Throws: R
Height: 6'5" Weight: 230 Origin: Round 8, 2013 Draft (#240 overall)

YEAR	TEAM	LVL	AGE	W	L	SV	G	GS	IP	H	HR	BB/9	K/9	K	GB%	BABIP
2016	VIS	A+	20	9	7	0	24	24	135	147	13	1.7	6.6	99	56%	.321
2017	WTN	AA	21	10	9	0	26	26	130^2	142	7	3.9	7.6	111	51%	.339
2018	KCA	MLB	22	9	6	0	41	20	140^1	133	7	3.2	6.2	96	56%	.294
2019	KCA	MLB	23	9	11	0	28	28	159	164	19	3.2	6.7	118	51%	.299

Breakout: 20% Improve: 39% Collapse: 25% Attrition: 30% MLB: 77%
Comparables: Aaron Sanchez, Antonio Senzatela, Robert Gsellman

Hailing from the bucolic-sounding town of Flowery Branch, Georgia, Keller was nabbed by the Reds from Arizona in the 2018 Rule 5 draft and immediately flipped to the Royals. Once in Kansas City, his reliable ground-ball tendencies earned him a rotation spot by the end of May and made him the Royals' most valuable starter in the second half of the season. Keller's sinking fastball is designed not for whiffs but for downward contact, and while it's fair to be skeptical of the gaudy ERA, his profile suggests a solid mid-rotation arm in 2019 and beyond. The problem is that he might just be the Royals' best candidate for Opening Day starter.

YEAR	TEAM	LVL	AGE	WHIP	ERA	DRA	WARP	MPH	FB%	WHF	CSP
2016	VIS	A+	20	1.28	4.47	4.08	2.2				
2017	WTN	AA	21	1.52	4.68	4.07	1.7				
2018	KCA	MLB	22	1.30	3.08	4.87	0.6	96.1	69.8	9.8	46.5
2019	KCA	MLB	23	1.40	4.31	4.75	1.2	96.0	72.3	10.1	48.2

Kansas City Royals 2019

Brad Keller, continued

Pitch Shape vs LHH
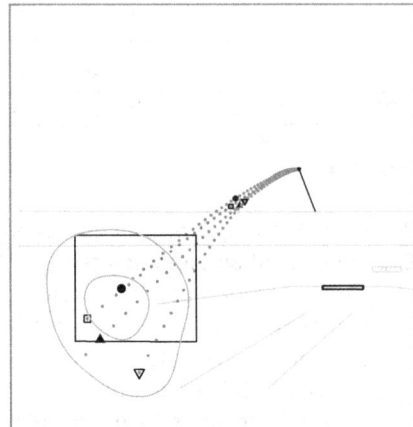

Pitch Shape vs RHH
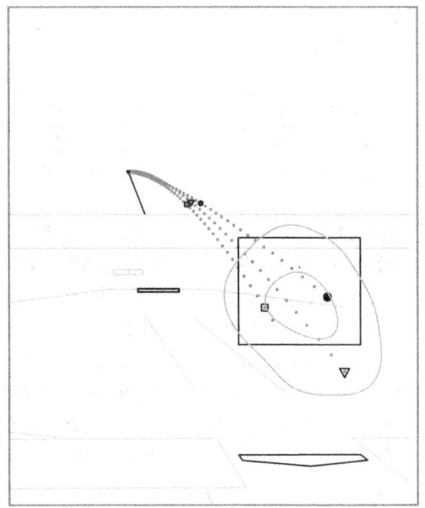

Type	Frequency	Velocity	H Movement	V Movement
● Fastball	44.3%	94.8 [107]	-0.4 [129]	-14.8 [103]
☐ Sinker	25.5%	93.6 [105]	-9.7 [124]	-19 [105]
+ Cutter				
▲ Changeup	4.1%	88.8 [114]	-9.4 [110]	-24.7 [108]
× Splitter				
▽ Slider	26.2%	85.9 [107]	5.7 [103]	-35.3 [93]
◇ Curveball				
⊕ Slow Curveball				
✳ Knuckleball				
▼ Screwball				

Ian Kennedy RHP
Born: 12/19/84   Age: 34   Bats: R   Throws: R
Height: 6'0"   Weight: 205   Origin: Round 1, 2006 Draft (#21 overall)

YEAR	TEAM	LVL	AGE	W	L	SV	G	GS	IP	H	HR	BB/9	K/9	K	GB%	BABIP
2016	KCA	MLB	31	11	11	0	33	33	195^2	173	33	3.0	8.5	184	34%	.268
2017	KCA	MLB	32	5	13	0	30	30	154	143	34	3.6	7.7	131	36%	.257
2018	KCA	MLB	33	3	9	0	22	22	119^2	125	20	3.0	7.9	105	31%	.298
2019	KCA	MLB	34	7	12	0	27	27	153	165	31	3.4	7.2	123	35%	.292

Breakout: 17%   Improve: 49%   Collapse: 13%   Attrition: 11%   MLB: 81%
Comparables: Aaron Harang, Earl Wilson, Jerry Koosman

There's no easier sport in the world than playing 20/20 hindsight with long-term free-agent contracts for pitchers in their early thirties coming off a down season and no sustained record of consistency, but you didn't need a modded-out DeLorean to see how this one would end up. Arriving in KC in 2016, just in time to experience the championship hangover without any of the champagne showers, Kennedy has labored to a total of one (one!) WARP across the first three seasons of a five (five!) year contract. The question isn't really whether he'll recoup any value, but whether it's possible for one pitcher to single-handedly reverse Kauffman's long-standing position as one of the more homer-unfriendly environments in the majors.

YEAR	TEAM	LVL	AGE	WHIP	ERA	DRA	WARP	MPH	FB%	WHF	CSP
2016	KCA	MLB	31	1.22	3.68	4.93	1.0	94.5	66.2	11.1	48
2017	KCA	MLB	32	1.32	5.38	6.18	-1.0	93.6	61.7	10.2	50.2
2018	KCA	MLB	33	1.38	4.66	5.32	0.0	93.7	58.7	9	49.2
2019	KCA	MLB	34	1.45	5.29	5.80	-0.7	92.8	61.2	9.9	48.5

Kansas City Royals 2019

Ian Kennedy, continued

Pitch Shape vs LHH

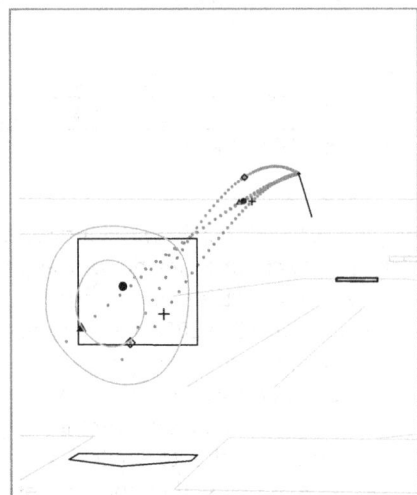

Pitch Shape vs RHH

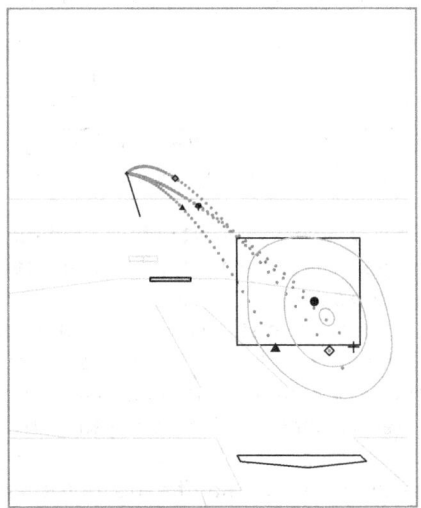

Type	Frequency	Velocity	H Movement	V Movement
● Fastball	58.2%	92.4 [100]	-7.3 [97]	-13.1 [108]
☐ Sinker	0.5%	92.4 [99]	-13.8 [91]	-18.2 [107]
+ Cutter	11.8%	88.1 [96]	1.6 [98]	-24.4 [97]
▲ Changeup	10.2%	85.6 [101]	-10.9 [102]	-22.6 [114]
✕ Splitter				
▽ Slider				
◇ Curveball	19.4%	78.7 [101]	9 [105]	-51.7 [92]
⊕ Slow Curveball				
✳ Knuckleball				
▼ Screwball				

Jorge Lopez RHP

Born: 02/10/93 Age: 26 Bats: R Throws: R
Height: 6'3" Weight: 195 Origin: Round 2, 2011 Draft (#70 overall)

YEAR	TEAM	LVL	AGE	W	L	SV	G	GS	IP	H	HR	BB/9	K/9	K	GB%	BABIP
2016	CSP	AAA	23	1	7	0	17	16	79^1	101	12	6.2	7.5	66	58%	.355
2016	BLX	AA	23	2	4	0	8	8	45^1	45	5	3.2	9.3	47	48%	.323
2017	MIL	MLB	24	0	0	0	1	0	2	4	0	4.5	0.0	0	44%	.444
2017	BLX	AA	24	8	8	7	39	13	103^2	92	7	3.3	9.1	105	49%	.301
2018	CSP	AAA	25	3	3	5	24	0	28^2	33	3	3.1	7.2	23	63%	.333
2018	MIL	MLB	25	0	1	0	10	0	19^2	16	1	5.9	6.9	15	56%	.268
2018	OMA	AAA	25	1	0	0	2	2	9	8	2	1.0	11.0	11	26%	.286
2018	KCA	MLB	25	2	4	0	7	7	34	41	5	2.4	6.1	23	40%	.324
2019	KCA	MLB	26	6	8	0	57	16	123	130	16	4.2	7.2	99	48%	.302

Breakout: 22%   Improve: 36%   Collapse: 15%   Attrition: 25%   MLB: 68%
Comparables: Clay Hensley, Bryan Mitchell, Rafael Montero

In dealing Mike Moustakas, the Royals did something that may prove to be sneaky smart; rather than getting back high-upside prospects who were years away from big-league contribution, they got two distressed assets who were potentially close to major-league contribution. While there was some prospect fatigue with former top-100 outfielder Brett Phillips, Lopez, the other piece in the trade, had been battered and bruised by the thin air of Colorado Springs, the unfortunately-chosen Triple-A outlet of the Brewers (and a city which has since been demoted to Rookie League affiliation). Lopez features a fringy fastball but excellent command of secondary pitches, including a plus curveball—precisely the profile to generate a 6.52 ERA across a season and a half with the Sky Sox. Some late-season work with the Royals proved inconclusive, but the lower-altitude Lopez should get a chance at a career reset in 2019.

YEAR	TEAM	LVL	AGE	WHIP	ERA	DRA	WARP	MPH	FB%	WHF	CSP
2016	CSP	AAA	23	1.97	6.81	7.06	-1.6				
2016	BLX	AA	23	1.35	3.97	3.94	0.6				
2017	MIL	MLB	24	2.50	4.50	9.45	-0.1	96.1	74.3	5.7	42.2
2017	BLX	AA	24	1.25	4.25	3.33	2.1				
2018	CSP	AAA	25	1.50	5.65	4.23	0.3				
2018	MIL	MLB	25	1.47	2.75	3.84	0.3	95.6	53.5	11.5	43.8
2018	OMA	AAA	25	1.00	4.00	2.83	0.2				
2018	KCA	MLB	25	1.47	6.35	5.08	0.0	95.2	50.8	7.4	51.1
2019	KCA	MLB	26	1.52	4.83	5.15	0.3	95.0	53.4	8.9	46.5

Jorge Lopez, continued

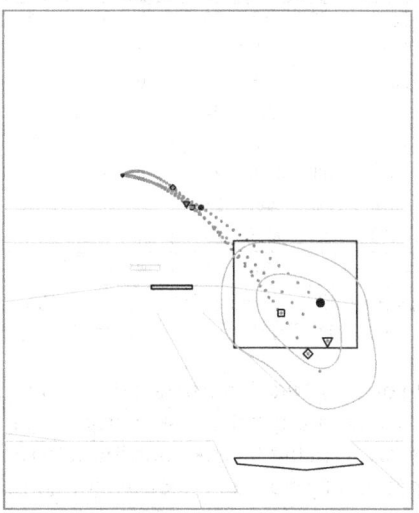

Type		Frequency	Velocity	H Movement	V Movement
●	Fastball	21.1%	94.5 [106]	-7.4 [96]	-14.8 [103]
□	Sinker	30.6%	94 [108]	-14 [88]	-19.5 [103]
+	Cutter				
▲	Changeup	11.0%	88.2 [112]	-12.9 [91]	-26.5 [102]
×	Splitter				
▽	Slider	10.5%	87.8 [115]	2.8 [91]	-27.2 [117]
◇	Curveball	26.8%	81.6 [112]	6 [92]	-46.4 [104]
✦	Slow Curveball				
✳	Knuckleball				
▼	Screwball				

Kevin McCarthy RHP

Born: 02/22/92 Age: 27 Bats: R Throws: R
Height: 6'3" Weight: 215 Origin: Round 16, 2013 Draft (#474 overall)

YEAR	TEAM	LVL	AGE	W	L	SV	G	GS	IP	H	HR	BB/9	K/9	K	GB%	BABIP
2016	NWA	AA	24	3	2	11	22	0	34^2	26	3	2.1	7.5	29	53%	.245
2016	OMA	AAA	24	2	4	5	25	0	33^1	28	4	4.3	8.1	30	56%	.270
2016	KCA	MLB	24	1	0	0	10	0	8^1	11	1	5.4	7.6	7	55%	.357
2017	OMA	AAA	25	1	1	2	25	0	32	32	3	2.5	4.8	17	58%	.296
2017	KCA	MLB	25	1	0	0	33	0	45	50	4	2.6	5.4	27	55%	.303
2018	KCA	MLB	26	5	4	0	65	0	72	70	7	2.5	5.8	46	65%	.289
2019	KCA	MLB	27	3	3	0	52	0	54^2	55	5	3.6	6.3	39	54%	.294

Breakout: 20%   Improve: 40%   Collapse: 20%   Attrition: 23%   MLB: 71%
Comparables: Ramon Troncoso, Franquelis Osoria, Ryan Webb

The answer to the never-to-be-asked trivia question, "Who was the 2018 Royals best reliever by BWARP?," McCarthy managed an impressively anonymous season of steady, unspectacular competence. Inducing ground-ball contact on nearly two-thirds of his hitters faced (which ranked him fourth in the majors among pitchers with at least 70 IP), McCarthy found a formula of sorts to become one of the only reliable arms in an otherwise shaky pen. His sinker/change combo is built for contact rather than strikeouts, however, which suggests a return to a middle-inning role.

YEAR	TEAM	LVL	AGE	WHIP	ERA	DRA	WARP	MPH	FB%	WHF	CSP
2016	NWA	AA	24	0.98	3.12	2.97	0.7				
2016	OMA	AAA	24	1.32	2.97	3.85	0.4				
2016	KCA	MLB	24	1.92	6.48	7.59	-0.2	96.1	61.5	4.8	48.5
2017	OMA	AAA	25	1.28	3.09	4.04	0.4				
2017	KCA	MLB	25	1.40	3.20	5.36	-0.1	94.3	60.8	9.7	52.3
2018	KCA	MLB	26	1.25	3.25	4.46	0.4	93.4	67	10.1	49.4
2019	KCA	MLB	27	1.42	4.42	4.71	0.3	93.3	65.3	9.8	50.7

Kansas City Royals 2019

Kevin McCarthy, continued

Pitch Shape vs LHH **Pitch Shape vs RHH**

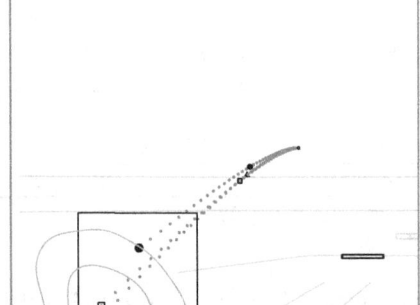
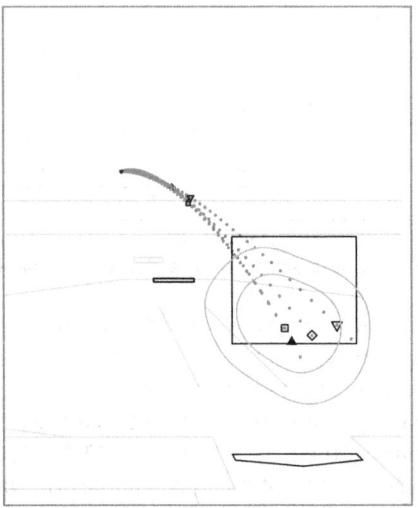

Type	Frequency	Velocity	H Movement	V Movement
● Fastball	5.6%	92.3 [99]	-7.9 [95]	-17.4 [95]
☐ Sinker	61.4%	92.2 [99]	-12 [105]	-24.2 [87]
+ Cutter				
▲ Changeup	22.1%	84.9 [98]	-13 [91]	-29.8 [93]
✕ Splitter				
▽ Slider	6.5%	86.9 [111]	1.1 [84]	-27.7 [116]
◇ Curveball	4.4%	82.9 [116]	5.6 [91]	-35.6 [128]
⊕ Slow Curveball				
✳ Knuckleball				
▼ Screwball				

Trevor Oaks RHP

Born: 03/26/93 Age: 26 Bats: R Throws: R
Height: 6'3" Weight: 225 Origin: Round 7, 2014 Draft (#219 overall)

YEAR	TEAM	LVL	AGE	W	L	SV	G	GS	IP	H	HR	BB/9	K/9	K	GB%	BABIP
2016	RCU	A+	23	1	1	0	4	4	25	26	1	1.1	7.9	22	60%	.352
2016	TUL	AA	23	8	1	0	10	10	63	56	1	1.3	5.4	38	65%	.276
2016	OKL	AAA	23	5	1	0	10	10	63	64	7	1.3	6.9	48	58%	.300
2017	OKL	AAA	24	4	3	0	16	15	84	87	5	1.9	7.7	72	52%	.336
2018	KCA	MLB	25	0	2	0	4	2	13^2	21	1	4.0	6.6	10	45%	.417
2018	OMA	AAA	25	8	8	0	22	22	128^1	130	5	3.1	4.9	70	51%	.298
2019	KCA	MLB	26	1	2	0	13	3	26	28	3	3.0	6.1	18	50%	.293

Breakout: 11% Improve: 21% Collapse: 14% Attrition: 26% MLB: 47%
Comparables: Jake Buchanan, Tyler Wagner, Myles Jaye

One of the few things a pitcher can do to push back on the entropy and decay that attends the forward motion of time's arrow is to learn a new pitch, or significantly alter an existing one. Oaks, working with former major-leaguers Justin Masterson and some dude named Greg Maddux, modified his bread-and-butter sinker to return to the elite ground-ball rates he posted before an oblique injury cost him most of 2017. While the 2018 results were good at Triple-A, and earned him a few innings in the show, his only path to major-league relevance is by pitching to contact, and if that contact isn't both weak and downward, Oaks' career path will be.

YEAR	TEAM	LVL	AGE	WHIP	ERA	DRA	WARP	MPH	FB%	WHF	CSP
2016	RCU	A+	23	1.16	3.60	3.28	0.6				
2016	TUL	AA	23	1.03	2.14	2.99	1.6				
2016	OKL	AAA	23	1.16	3.00	3.50	1.3				
2017	OKL	AAA	24	1.25	3.64	4.07	1.5				
2018	KCA	MLB	25	1.98	7.24	5.48	0.0	91.1	58.7	11.7	47.1
2018	OMA	AAA	25	1.36	3.23	5.40	0.2				
2019	KCA	MLB	26	1.37	4.55	4.90	0.1	90.7	59.8	12	47.9

Kansas City Royals 2019

Trevor Oaks, continued

Pitch Shape vs LHH

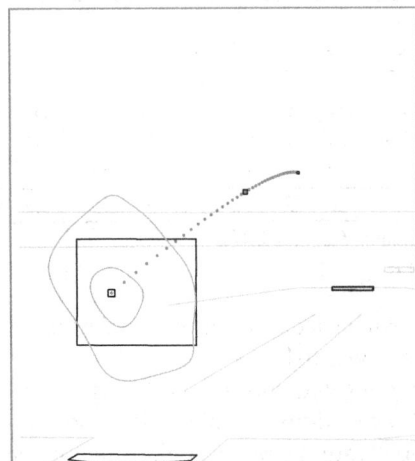

Pitch Shape vs RHH

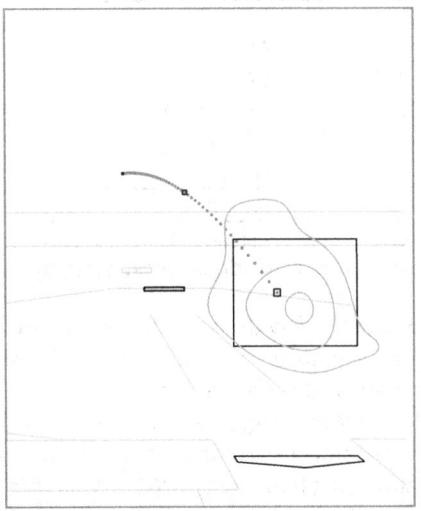

Type	Frequency	Velocity	H Movement	V Movement
● Fastball	4.9%	90.9 [95]	-5.8 [104]	-17.7 [94]
□ Sinker	53.8%	90.1 [88]	-12.1 [104]	-23.3 [90]
+ Cutter	14.2%	86.4 [86]	-0.6 [85]	-27.6 [85]
▲ Changeup	4.0%	83.2 [92]	-13 [91]	-26.6 [102]
× Splitter				
▽ Slider	23.1%	82.4 [91]	3.6 [95]	-34.4 [96]
◇ Curveball				
⊕ Slow Curveball				
✴ Knuckleball				
▼ Screwball				

Wily Peralta RHP

Born: 05/08/89   Age: 30   Bats: R   Throws: R
Height: 6'1"   Weight: 255   Origin: International Free Agent, 2005

YEAR	TEAM	LVL	AGE	W	L	SV	G	GS	IP	H	HR	BB/9	K/9	K	GB%	BABIP
2016	CSP	AAA	27	1	3	0	10	10	41^1	55	5	3.7	8.5	39	56%	.391
2016	MIL	MLB	27	7	11	0	23	23	127^2	152	19	3.0	6.6	93	52%	.336
2017	MIL	MLB	28	5	4	0	19	8	57^1	73	10	5.0	8.2	52	46%	.362
2017	CSP	AAA	28	1	0	1	13	0	16	13	0	5.6	5.6	10	57%	.255
2018	OMA	AAA	29	0	1	1	18	2	35	36	3	5.4	10.0	39	57%	.351
2018	KCA	MLB	29	1	0	14	37	0	34^1	28	4	6.0	9.2	35	49%	.279
2019	KCA	MLB	30	3	2	18	52	0	54^2	49	4	4.4	8.6	52	49%	.301

Breakout: 18%   Improve: 53%   Collapse: 13%   Attrition: 12%   MLB: 83%
Comparables: Victor Santos, Dillon Gee, Ross Detwiler

For a bad team, the last few months of a baseball season must be a weird time. Summer drags on interminably; everyone has to find reasons to show up and care about making pitches, grinding out at bats, staying healthy, and generally trying to derive some purpose and pleasure from a game that must feel like a clock-punching exercise. For Peralta, earning and keeping the rarefied title of "major-league closer" may have held some motivation. By this criterion, Peralta was perfect: 14 save chances, all converted (the only other pitcher with more than ten saves not to blow a chance in 2018? Ken Giles). Peralta still walked far too many batters, and his role would likely have come under scrutiny on a team with more at stake, but for the Royals in 2018, the unblemished results were enough to transform him into a capital-C Closer and give him the inside track to continue the role in 2019.

YEAR	TEAM	LVL	AGE	WHIP	ERA	DRA	WARP	MPH	FB%	WHF	CSP
2016	CSP	AAA	27	1.74	6.31	4.92	0.2				
2016	MIL	MLB	27	1.53	4.86	5.82	-0.7	97.6	62.7	9.4	41.5
2017	MIL	MLB	28	1.83	7.85	7.18	-1.1	97.8	58.4	9.3	42.4
2017	CSP	AAA	28	1.44	3.38	4.84	0.1				
2018	OMA	AAA	29	1.63	4.37	3.70	0.6				
2018	KCA	MLB	29	1.49	3.67	6.24	-0.5	97.8	49.6	10.5	43.7
2019	KCA	MLB	30	1.41	3.55	3.99	0.7	96.9	58.3	9.6	42.6

Kansas City Royals 2019

Wily Peralta, continued

Pitch Shape vs LHH

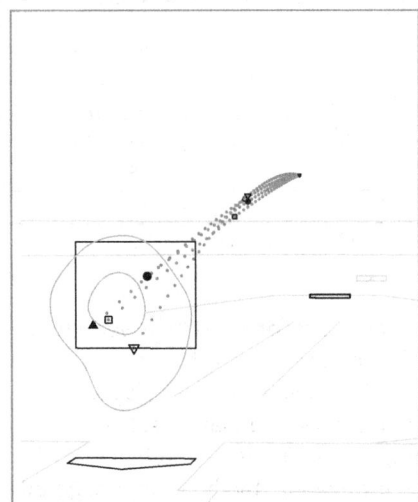

Pitch Shape vs RHH

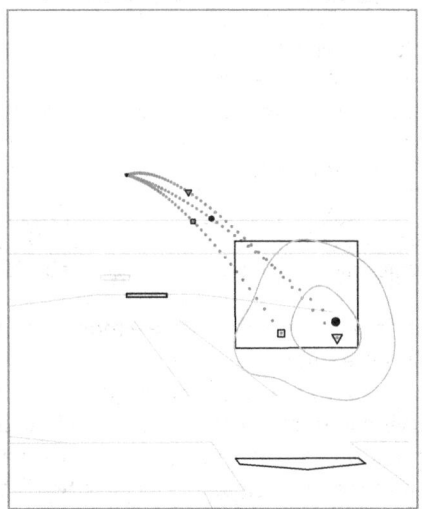

Type	Frequency	Velocity	H Movement	V Movement
● Fastball	25.0%	96.9 [114]	-7.1 [98]	-12.6 [110]
☐ Sinker	24.6%	96.3 [119]	-9.6 [125]	-14.8 [118]
+ Cutter				
▲ Changeup	11.1%	86.6 [105]	-10.2 [106]	-24.2 [109]
× Splitter				
▽ Slider	39.3%	84.1 [98]	1.2 [84]	-35.6 [92]
◇ Curveball				
⊕ Slow Curveball				
✷ Knuckleball				
▼ Screwball				

Eric Skoglund LHP

Born: 10/26/92 Age: 26 Bats: L Throws: L
Height: 6'7" Weight: 210 Origin: Round 3, 2014 Draft (#92 overall)

YEAR	TEAM	LVL	AGE	W	L	SV	G	GS	IP	H	HR	BB/9	K/9	K	GB%	BABIP
2016	NWA	AA	23	7	10	0	27	27	156^1	135	19	2.2	7.7	134	44%	.263
2017	OMA	AAA	24	4	5	0	19	19	100^2	110	14	2.6	9.1	102	42%	.331
2017	KCA	MLB	24	1	2	0	7	5	18	30	2	6.0	7.0	14	39%	.431
2018	KCA	MLB	25	1	6	0	14	13	70	66	12	2.4	6.3	49	44%	.261
2019	KCA	MLB	26	3	4	0	18	8	56	60	9	3.1	6.7	42	42%	.294

Breakout: 20% Improve: 38% Collapse: 29% Attrition: 39% MLB: 77%
Comparables: Marco Gonzales, Parker Bridwell, A.J. Cole

One thing that defines the current pitching epoch: tall, skinny lefties will find work beyond the point where skill level ceases to merit continued employment. OK, that's been true since the dawn of the La Russa bullpen, but now those guys are starting, too. Maybe something about the visual echoes of Sale, Kershaw, and Hader work unconsciously on scouts, GMs and managers to project glimmers of something great where there is mere competence. This is just a theory, but it's one that may be tested by the role Skoglund assumes in 2019. The average fastball, low strikeout rates and home-run propensity put him in a very large and crowded bucket with other potential fifth-starter pieces in Kansas City, but everyone loves a limb-shaking southpaw, and Skoglund may well be chosen for rotation duty simply because Ned Yost can't see who's standing behind him.

YEAR	TEAM	LVL	AGE	WHIP	ERA	DRA	WARP	MPH	FB%	WHF	CSP
2016	NWA	AA	23	1.11	3.45	3.31	3.4				
2017	OMA	AAA	24	1.38	4.11	3.75	2.2				
2017	KCA	MLB	24	2.33	9.50	8.05	-0.5	94.1	63.3	7.1	54
2018	KCA	MLB	25	1.21	5.14	6.20	-0.7	93.4	60.2	8	49.2
2019	KCA	MLB	26	1.40	4.83	5.20	0.1	93.1	62	8	52.2

Kansas City Royals 2019

Eric Skoglund, continued

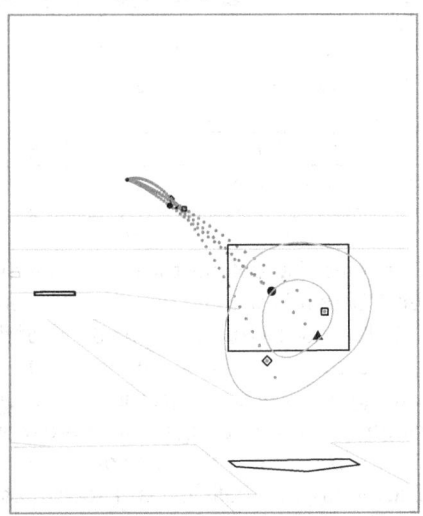

Type	Frequency	Velocity	H Movement	V Movement
● Fastball	30.7%	92 [98]	9.1 [89]	14.4 [104]
☐ Sinker	29.5%	92 [97]	13.7 [91]	-19.1 [104]
+ Cutter				
▲ Changeup	13.6%	86.2 [103]	10.6 [104]	-24.1 [109]
✕ Splitter				
▽ Slider	1.9%	83 [94]	-3.7 [95]	-38 [85]
◇ Curveball	24.3%	81.7 [112]	-3.5 [82]	-39.6 [119]
⊕ Slow Curveball				
✴ Knuckleball				
▼ Screwball				

Glenn Sparkman RHP

Born: 05/11/92 Age: 27 Bats: B Throws: R
Height: 6'2" Weight: 210 Origin: Round 20, 2013 Draft (#594 overall)

YEAR	TEAM	LVL	AGE	W	L	SV	G	GS	IP	H	HR	BB/9	K/9	K	GB%	BABIP
2016	ROY	RK	24	1	3	0	7	7	16²	19	1	0.5	9.2	17	56%	.353
2016	LEX	A	24	0	2	0	3	3	14¹	21	2	1.9	11.9	19	46%	.487
2016	WIL	A+	24	1	0	0	2	2	11²	9	1	0.8	6.9	9	46%	.235
2016	NWA	AA	24	0	2	0	4	4	17²	21	2	2.5	10.2	20	30%	.373
2017	TOR	MLB	25	0	0	0	2	0	1	9	0	9.0	9.0	1	20%	.900
2018	NWA	AA	26	3	2	0	6	6	33²	35	0	0.3	7.0	26	45%	.321
2018	OMA	AAA	26	5	1	0	12	12	67¹	76	10	1.5	6.4	48	46%	.314
2018	KCA	MLB	26	0	3	0	15	3	38¹	47	3	3.5	6.3	27	47%	.338
2019	KCA	MLB	27	0	0	0	10	0	10	12	2	3.3	6.8	8	43%	.294

Breakout: 12%   Improve: 16%   Collapse: 32%   Attrition: 38%   MLB: 66%
Comparables: Sean Gilmartin, Cody Martin, Eric Surkamp

The Rule 5 draft is a garage sale with a very liberal return policy. We all know about those Rule 5 picks who go on to great success: Dan Uggla. Johan Santana. Jose Bautista. R.A. Dickey. But what about the players returned to their original teams? How does a used suit feel when it doesn't even merit the forgotten spot at the dark end of the closet? After suffering a broken thumb in the spring of 2017, Sparkman was returned from the Blue Jays to the Royals. He worked his way into a midseason call-up in 2018 and did what swing men are built to do: ate some innings in blowout losses and earned a few starts when pitchers (Danny Duffy, in this instance) were sidelined. Sparkman has decent control, mid-90s velocity, and ground-ball tendencies, all of which are useful but none of which are exceptional enough to lift him out of swingman purgatory, or into a guaranteed job.

YEAR	TEAM	LVL	AGE	WHIP	ERA	DRA	WARP	MPH	FB%	WHF	CSP
2016	ROY	RK	24	1.20	5.40	3.10	0.5				
2016	LEX	A	24	1.67	6.91	2.65	0.4				
2016	WIL	A+	24	0.86	3.86	3.62	0.2				
2016	NWA	AA	24	1.47	4.58	2.59	0.5				
2017	TOR	MLB	25	10.00	63.00	9.33	0.0	95.2	63.6	3.6	46.8
2018	NWA	AA	26	1.07	2.94	4.47	0.3				
2018	OMA	AAA	26	1.29	4.01	3.74	1.4				
2018	KCA	MLB	26	1.62	4.46	5.21	-0.1	95.9	56.6	10.6	48.9
2019	KCA	MLB	27	1.43	4.98	5.13	0.0	95.4	57.7	10.3	48.6

Kansas City Royals 2019

Glenn Sparkman, continued

Pitch Shape vs LHH

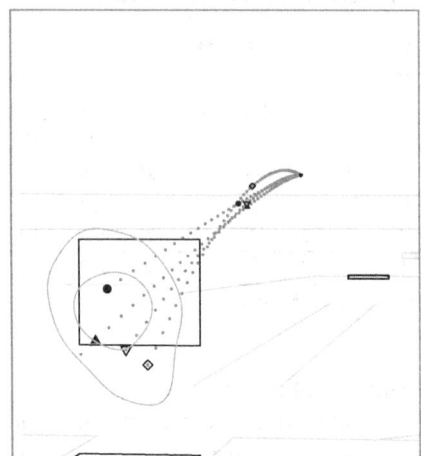

Pitch Shape vs RHH

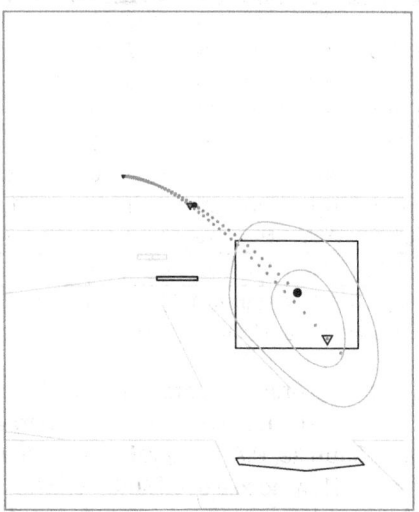

Type	Frequency	Velocity	H Movement	V Movement
● Fastball	56.6%	94.3 [106]	-8.7 [90]	-14.4 [104]
☐ Sinker				
+ Cutter				
▲ Changeup	9.9%	85.7 [101]	-12.9 [91]	-23.6 [111]
✕ Splitter				
▽ Slider	25.2%	86.8 [111]	0.6 [81]	-27.2 [117]
◇ Curveball	8.4%	80.4 [107]	6.1 [93]	-49.5 [97]
⊕ Slow Curveball				
✳ Knuckleball				
▼ Screwball				

Terrance Gore LF

Born: 06/08/91 Age: 28 Bats: R Throws: R
Height: 5'7" Weight: 165 Origin: Round 20, 2011 Draft (#606 overall)

YEAR	TEAM	LVL	AGE	PA	R	2B	3B	HR	RBI	BB	K	SB	CS	AVG/OBP/SLG
2016	NWA	AA	25	302	31	2	1	0	11	26	58	44	5	.233/.314/.249
2016	KCA	MLB	25	3	6	0	0	0	0	0	1	11	2	.000/.000/.000
2017	NWA	AA	26	62	9	1	0	0	1	2	13	8	0	.254/.279/.271
2017	OMA	AAA	26	192	29	3	3	1	10	16	38	13	3	.247/.321/.319
2017	KCA	MLB	26	5	2	0	0	0	0	1	2	2	2	.000/.200/.000
2018	OMA	AAA	27	168	26	2	2	0	5	17	36	16	4	.211/.304/.254
2018	IOW	AAA	27	37	6	0	0	0	0	2	13	5	1	.118/.189/.118
2018	CHN	MLB	27	5	5	0	0	0	0	0	1	6	0	.200/.200/.200
2019	KCA	MLB	28	251	30	3	1	4	18	14	59	20	3	.212/.263/.292

Breakout: 3% Improve: 18% Collapse: 1% Attrition: 17% MLB: 25%
Comparables: Luis Durango, Norris Hopper, Freddy Guzman

It's possible that Gore is both the best runner and worst hitter in pro ball. The Wild Card game was a microcosm of his utility, or lack thereof: he saved the Cubs from elimination in the eighth inning, stealing second and then hurtling home to tie the game on a single. In other words, Gore did exactly what he was there for. The problem was that the Cubs ran out of position players to replace him with, and so once again needing a single run to save their season in the bottom of the 13th, Gore was thrust back into the spotlight, this time with a bat in his hand. Gore's skillset represents a very specific tool that is monumentally useful in playoff baseball if deployed at the right time. At any other, it's like using a rubber duck when you need a hammer.

YEAR	TEAM	LVL	AGE	PA	DRC+	VORP	BABIP	BRR	FRAA	WARP
2016	NWA	AA	25	302	66	5.7	.303	5.4	CF(70): 5.2, LF(15): -0.1	0.4
2016	KCA	MLB	25	3	87	-0.5	.000	0.1	LF(2): 0.0	0.0
2017	NWA	AA	26	62	58	-1.2	.326	1.4	LF(10): 1.5, CF(7): -0.3	0.0
2017	OMA	AAA	26	192	65	2.4	.310	2.5	LF(30): 1.1, CF(29): 0.7	0.0
2017	KCA	MLB	26	5	70	-0.4	.000	0.3	LF(2): -0.2	0.0
2018	OMA	AAA	27	168	39	-1.4	.283	2.0	LF(42): -0.2, CF(18): 1.4	-0.6
2018	IOW	AAA	27	37	36	-3.8	.190	0.7	CF(6): -0.5, LF(5): -0.4	-0.2
2018	CHN	MLB	27	5	79	0.2	.250	0.9	LF(7): -0.2	0.1
2019	KCA	MLB	28	251	44	-5.4	.254	3.4	LF 2, CF 2	-0.1

Kyle Isbel CF

Born: 03/03/97   Age: 22   Bats: L   Throws: R
Height: 5'11"   Weight: 183   Origin: Round 3, 2018 Draft (#94 overall)

YEAR	TEAM	LVL	AGE	PA	R	2B	3B	HR	RBI	BB	K	SB	CS	AVG/OBP/SLG
2018	IDA	RK	21	119	27	10	1	4	18	14	17	12	3	.381/.454/.610
2018	LEX	A	21	174	30	12	1	3	14	12	43	12	3	.289/.345/.434
2019	KCA	MLB	22	251	27	12	0	6	21	6	77	7	2	.191/.210/.315

Breakout: 4%   Improve: 4%   Collapse: 0%   Attrition: 4%   MLB: 5%
Comparables: Darrell Ceciliani, Roger Bernadina, Xavier Avery

A bit undersized and perhaps destined for a corner outfield or second-base home, former UNLV center fielder Isbel did his best to justify his spot as the Royals' highest-drafted position player from the 2018 class. After ripping through the Northwest League, he finished the season at Low-A Lexington, where he continued to hit hard, run fast, and (in true Royals prospect tradition) swing often. There seem to be few roadblocks in Isbel's way as he hopes to do some drive-by truckin' through multiple minor-league levels in 2019.

YEAR	TEAM	LVL	AGE	PA	DRC+	VORP	BABIP	BRR	FRAA	WARP
2018	IDA	RK	21	119	195	18.0	.429	-0.8	CF(19): 4.5, RF(2): 1.1	1.6
2018	LEX	A	21	174	110	7.0	.377	2.8	CF(27): 0.8, LF(11): -0.5	0.7
2019	KCA	MLB	22	251	38	-9.1	.247	0.7	CF 2, LF 0	-0.8

Khalil Lee CF

Born: 06/26/98 Age: 21 Bats: L Throws: L
Height: 5'10" Weight: 170 Origin: Round 3, 2016 Draft (#103 overall)

YEAR	TEAM	LVL	AGE	PA	R	2B	3B	HR	RBI	BB	K	SB	CS	AVG/OBP/SLG
2016	ROY	RK	18	222	43	9	6	6	29	33	57	8	4	.269/.396/.484
2017	LEX	A	19	532	71	24	6	17	61	65	171	20	18	.237/.344/.430
2018	WIL	A+	20	301	42	13	4	4	41	48	75	14	3	.270/.402/.406
2018	NWA	AA	20	118	15	5	0	2	10	11	28	2	2	.245/.330/.353
2019	KCA	MLB	21	251	23	6	1	7	23	19	90	4	2	.150/.221/.271

Breakout: 4% Improve: 9% Collapse: 0% Attrition: 5% MLB: 9%
Comparables: Clint Frazier, Daniel Fields, Brandon Nimmo

Twenty-year-olds can go in so many different directions—that applies generally, but even more specifically to power-speed prospects. Lee flashed impressive amounts of both at Low-A but seemed to lose the power stroke at High-A Wilmington in 2018. Set to begin his age-21 season at Double-A, Lee has a future that is bright but not particularly clear. His plate approach still walks the line between patient and over-patient. Does the body fill out to 20-home-run power? Do the on-base skills mesh with the speed to create a run-scoring force? Or does the swing-and-miss begin to take center stage, dragging down the multi-tool upside? This should be the year when Lee's Magic 8-Ball comes up with something other than "Reply Hazy, Try Again."

YEAR	TEAM	LVL	AGE	PA	DRC+	VORP	BABIP	BRR	FRAA	WARP
2016	ROY	RK	18	222	131	18.6	.358	-0.4	CF(23): -2.5, RF(15): -2.5	-0.3
2017	LEX	A	19	532	109	20.1	.338	-2.2	CF(67): -6.2, RF(52): 4.3	0.6
2018	WIL	A+	20	301	140	26.4	.371	2.2	CF(57): 3.8, RF(9): 0.3	2.2
2018	NWA	AA	20	118	82	1.2	.319	0.6	CF(17): 0.3, LF(9): 0.7	0.0
2019	KCA	MLB	21	251	35	-10.7	.207	0.0	CF -2, RF 0	-1.4

Nicky Lopez MI

Born: 03/13/95 Age: 24 Bats: L Throws: R
Height: 5'11" Weight: 175 Origin: Round 5, 2016 Draft (#163 overall)

YEAR	TEAM	LVL	AGE	PA	R	2B	3B	HR	RBI	BB	K	SB	CS	AVG/OBP/SLG
2016	BNC	RK	21	283	54	6	5	6	29	35	30	24	4	.281/.393/.429
2017	WIL	A+	22	324	42	12	7	2	27	36	23	14	8	.295/.376/.407
2017	NWA	AA	22	253	26	6	1	0	11	16	29	7	4	.259/.312/.293
2018	NWA	AA	23	325	42	8	5	2	27	33	23	9	4	.331/.397/.416
2018	OMA	AAA	23	256	33	6	2	7	26	27	29	6	2	.278/.364/.417
2019	KCA	MLB	24	105	11	2	1	2	10	7	14	2	1	.242/.298/.347

Breakout: 16% Improve: 28% Collapse: 1% Attrition: 24% MLB: 43%
Comparables: Kevin Newman, Tony Kemp, Greg Garcia

Bad problems to have: Unidentified dark fluid pooling under your car engine. A power outage with a freezer full of fresh game. A rash only made worse by over-the-counter medication. Going the wrong way over tire spikes. Spotty internet when you just pressed "purchase now." That "stomach thing" going around your child's first-grade class. An upstairs neighbor who never got beyond his nu-metal phase. A paucity of middle-infield talent in your organization.
Good problems to have: A litter of cute puppies. A weekend with perfect weather and nothing to do. Frequent-flier miles that you need to use or lose. Halloween candy. A major-league-ready middle-infield prospect whose only apparent drawback is a lack of power, and a franchise building block who won't hit free agency until 2023.

YEAR	TEAM	LVL	AGE	PA	DRC+	VORP	BABIP	BRR	FRAA	WARP
2016	BNC	RK	21	283	151	34.1	.296	5.4	SS(62): 7.8	2.9
2017	WIL	A+	22	324	126	26.0	.315	0.8	SS(66): 4.4	2.1
2017	NWA	AA	22	253	74	4.5	.296	2.2	SS(33): -2.9, 2B(25): 2.5	-0.2
2018	NWA	AA	23	325	124	25.9	.351	2.8	SS(58): -4.8, 2B(14): 0.4	1.2
2018	OMA	AAA	23	256	120	19.5	.294	0.0	SS(36): -1.0, 2B(18): 1.7	1.3
2019	KCA	MLB	24	105	90	2.4	.266	0.1	SS 0, 3B 0	0.3

Seuly Matias RF
Born: 09/04/98   Age: 20   Bats: R   Throws: R
Height: 6'3"   Weight: 200   Origin: International Free Agent, 2015

YEAR	TEAM	LVL	AGE	PA	R	2B	3B	HR	RBI	BB	K	SB	CS	AVG/OBP/SLG
2016	DRY	RK	17	27	2	1	0	0	2	2	13	0	0	.125/.222/.167
2016	ROY	RK	17	198	32	11	2	8	29	22	73	2	4	.250/.348/.477
2017	BNC	RK	18	246	27	13	3	7	36	16	72	2	1	.243/.297/.423
2018	LEX	A	19	376	62	13	1	31	63	24	131	6	0	.231/.303/.550
2019	KCA	MLB	20	251	18	6	0	10	28	4	113	0	0	.122/.135/.273

Breakout: 20%   Improve: 24%   Collapse: 0%   Attrition: 4%   MLB: 24%
Comparables: Giancarlo Stanton, Domingo Santana, Cody Bellinger

Matias may be baseball's quality-control experiment as it tests just how much swing-and-miss a prospect can have while still succeeding on raw, brutal power. He clobbered Low-A as a 19-year-old, mashing a rich season's worth of home runs in a mere 376 plate appearances, with nearly identical strikeout and HR/FB rates in the mid-thirties. It helps Matias' case that he's an athletically-built right fielder with a cannon arm, so he should stick safely in the outfield. The question that Matias will pose: can a prospect make it on power alone even if that power is Straight Outta Stanton? Even Joey Gallo could take a walk now and again.

YEAR	TEAM	LVL	AGE	PA	DRC+	VORP	BABIP	BRR	FRAA	WARP
2016	DRY	RK	17	27	21	-1.4	.273	0.0	CF(6): 0.6, CF(1): 0.6	-0.1
2016	ROY	RK	17	198	101	9.9	.385	0.0	CF(23): -1.6, RF(19): 0.6	-0.3
2017	BNC	RK	18	246	81	7.0	.318	0.7	RF(52): 9.0	0.3
2018	LEX	A	19	376	96	18.8	.264	0.7	RF(75): -2.1	-0.4
2019	KCA	MLB	20	251	-4	-25.4	.158	-0.5	RF -1	-2.8

MJ Melendez C
Born: 11/29/98   Age: 20   Bats: L   Throws: R
Height: 6'1"   Weight: 185   Origin: Round 2, 2017 Draft (#52 overall)

YEAR	TEAM	LVL	AGE	PA	R	2B	3B	HR	RBI	BB	K	SB	CS	AVG/OBP/SLG
2017	ROY	RK	18	198	25	8	3	4	30	26	60	4	2	.262/.374/.417
2018	LEX	A	19	472	52	26	9	19	73	43	143	4	6	.251/.322/.492
2019	KCA	MLB	20	251	17	6	2	8	25	11	101	0	0	.130/.166/.265

Breakout: 5%   Improve: 7%   Collapse: 0%   Attrition: 4%   MLB: 7%
Comparables: Gary Sanchez, Matt Olson, Tommy Joseph

For all that has gone wrong with the Royals since 2015, things might be falling into place with respect to a worthy backstop successor to Sal Perez. Assuming that the hard-ridden Perez will loosen his death grip on the position sometime in the next half-decade, Melendez looks to be on a schedule that would deliver him to major-league relevance at the right time. A strong showing at Low-A suggests the power and defense are a worthy foundation; we'll have to wait and see how the hit tool comes along. But (CTRL+C, CTRL+V for every low-minors catching prospect) catchers, man. Who even knows?

YEAR	TEAM	LVL	AGE	PA	DRC+	VORP	BABIP	BRR	FRAA	WARP
2017	ROY	RK	18	198	117	11.4	.385	0.1	C(30): 0.5	0.2
2018	LEX	A	19	472	103	24.5	.327	-1.7	C(73): 1.4	0.8
2019	KCA	MLB	20	251	14	-15.6	.175	0.0	C 0	-1.7

Nick Pratto 1B

Born: 10/06/98 Age: 20 Bats: L Throws: L
Height: 6'1" Weight: 195 Origin: Round 1, 2017 Draft (#14 overall)

YEAR	TEAM	LVL	AGE	PA	R	2B	3B	HR	RBI	BB	K	SB	CS	AVG/OBP/SLG
2017	ROY	RK	18	230	25	15	3	4	34	24	58	10	4	.247/.330/.414
2018	LEX	A	19	537	79	33	2	14	62	45	150	22	5	.280/.343/.443
2019	KCA	MLB	20	251	20	10	0	6	24	8	90	3	1	.158/.183/.277

Breakout: 3% Improve: 5% Collapse: 0% Attrition: 3% MLB: 5%
Comparables: Jose Osuna, Chris Marrero, Dominic Smith

If you're going to be a first-base prospect, be a first-base prospect. Own it. Don't pretend you're a "third baseman who can make most of the throws" or a "left fielder who can cover most of the area"; just be the best doggone first-base prospect you can be. Pratto has never been anything but a first baseman, and this is not a veiled dig at defensive incompetence; he's a good first baseman. His 2018 season also hinted that he doesn't fall into the conventional slugger profile, displaying intriguing speed to go with gap power that should grow into more. As with nearly every Royals low-minors prospect, cutting down the strikeouts is the main challenge, but Pratto's advanced hit tool suggests that he might be better positioned than some of his organizational colleagues to meet it.

YEAR	TEAM	LVL	AGE	PA	DRC+	VORP	BABIP	BRR	FRAA	WARP
2017	ROY	RK	18	230	111	4.7	.319	-0.8	1B(51): 5.2	-0.1
2018	LEX	A	19	537	111	14.4	.375	1.4	1B(125): -0.6	0.3
2019	KCA	MLB	20	251	16	-20.7	.215	0.0	1B 1	-2.1

Meibrys Viloria C

Born: 02/15/97 Age: 22 Bats: L Throws: R
Height: 5'11" Weight: 220 Origin: International Free Agent, 2013

YEAR	TEAM	LVL	AGE	PA	R	2B	3B	HR	RBI	BB	K	SB	CS	AVG/OBP/SLG
2016	IDA	RK	19	259	54	28	3	6	55	20	36	1	1	.376/.436/.606
2017	LEX	A	20	398	42	25	0	8	52	25	79	4	3	.259/.313/.394
2018	WIL	A+	21	407	34	16	1	6	44	40	75	2	1	.260/.342/.360
2018	KCA	MLB	21	29	4	2	0	0	4	1	9	0	0	.259/.286/.333
2019	KCA	MLB	22	35	3	2	0	1	4	1	9	0	0	.212/.235/.364

Breakout: 9% Improve: 23% Collapse: 0% Attrition: 18% MLB: 26%
Comparables: Austin Hedges, Blake Swihart, John Ryan Murphy

Caught between the higher upside of M.J. Melendez and the major-league-backup readiness of Cam Gallagher, the Royals won't see much of Meibrys tomorrow but will they see Meibrys... someday? Viloria is on the 40-man roster and got a surprise September call-up after an age-appropriately decent year at High-A Wilmington, but he has not otherwise changed his place in this world. Of course, it never hurts to have extra young catchers in the organization, but Viloria may just be a Pretender to the throne that Sal Perez will eventually vacate.

YEAR	TEAM	P. COUNT	FRM RUNS	BLK RUNS	THRW RUNS	TOT RUNS
2018	KCA	1167	0.0	-0.8	0.0	-0.1
2019	KCA	1297	-0.1	-0.8	0.0	-0.9

YEAR	TEAM	LVL	AGE	PA	DRC+	VORP	BABIP	BRR	FRAA	WARP
2016	IDA	RK	19	259	174	39.5	.418	2.3	C(50): -0.8	2.3
2017	LEX	A	20	398	104	8.5	.310	-0.4	C(92): -0.4	1.2
2018	WIL	A+	21	407	107	11.0	.313	-2.8	C(88): 2.8	1.3
2018	KCA	MLB	21	29	74	0.2	.389	0.1	C(10): -1.0	0.0
2019	KCA	MLB	22	35	51	-0.5	.245	-0.1	C -1	-0.2

Scott Blewett RHP
Born: 04/10/96 Age: 23 Bats: R Throws: R
Height: 6'6" Weight: 210 Origin: Round 2, 2014 Draft (#56 overall)

YEAR	TEAM	LVL	AGE	W	L	SV	G	GS	IP	H	HR	BB/9	K/9	K	GB%	BABIP
2016	LEX	A	20	8	11	0	25	25	129^1	138	10	3.5	8.4	121	47%	.338
2017	WIL	A+	21	7	10	0	27	27	152^2	153	16	3.1	7.6	129	47%	.302
2018	NWA	AA	22	8	6	0	26	25	148^1	164	12	3.0	6.1	100	42%	.319
2019	*KCA*	*MLB*	*23*	*5*	*10*	*0*	*23*	*23*	*122*	*147*	*22*	*3.9*	*6.0*	*81*	*41%*	*.313*

Breakout: 5% Improve: 6% Collapse: 3% Attrition: 5% MLB: 11%
Comparables: Michael Lorenzen, Danny Salazar, David Buchanan

It's tough when you're a prospect whose growth is decelerating and your name is a past-tense homonym for failure. The clock is ticking, but the 23-year-old has a bit more time to prove that he can overcome the magnetic pull of nominative determinism. Still being thought of as a starter by the Royals, his changeup will have to develop into a credible third pitch alongside his fastball-curve combo if he is to fulfill that destiny. And if not, the life of a middle reliever isn't the worst life to live. He didn't make great strides at Double-A, but his youth, size, and fastball still keep him in the present-tense conversation, assuming you aren't reading this far in the future.

YEAR	TEAM	LVL	AGE	WHIP	ERA	DRA	WARP	MPH	FB%	WHF	CSP
2016	LEX	A	20	1.46	4.31	3.96	1.7				
2017	WIL	A+	21	1.34	4.07	5.24	0.0				
2018	NWA	AA	22	1.44	4.79	7.52	-3.8				
2019	*KCA*	*MLB*	*23*	*1.64*	*5.82*	*6.14*	*-0.9*				

Kris Bubic LHP

Born: 08/19/97 Age: 21 Bats: L Throws: L
Height: 6'3" Weight: 220 Origin: Round 1, 2018 Draft (#40 overall)

YEAR	TEAM	LVL	AGE	W	L	SV	G	GS	IP	H	HR	BB/9	K/9	K	GB%	BABIP
2018	IDA	RK	20	2	3	0	10	10	38	38	2	4.5	12.6	53	47%	.379
2019	KCA	MLB	21	1	3	0	7	7	30^2	33	4	7.4	8.1	28	44%	.317

Comparables: Thyago Vieira, Bryan Mitchell, Kendry Flores

Though it may get you noticed, a Kershaw-esque stop-start delivery alone will not get you drafted 40th overall. An effective fastball-change combo with an identical arm slot and repeatability will, apparently. Even if Bubic's ceiling is more Alex Wood than Clayton Kershaw, the Royals have cause to be excited for anyone in their system who bears passing resemblance to a mid-rotation starter, much less a multiple-Cy Young winner. The foundation is there for the Stanford product; a credible curveball is the main missing piece.

YEAR	TEAM	LVL	AGE	WHIP	ERA	DRA	WARP	MPH	FB%	WHF	CSP
2018	IDA	RK	20	1.50	4.03	2.95	1.3				
2019	KCA	MLB	21	1.89	5.92	6.23	-0.3				

Jesse Hahn RHP

Born: 07/30/89 Age: 29 Bats: R Throws: R
Height: 6'4" Weight: 215 Origin: Round 6, 2010 Draft (#191 overall)

YEAR	TEAM	LVL	AGE	W	L	SV	G	GS	IP	H	HR	BB/9	K/9	K	GB%	BABIP
2016	OAK	MLB	26	2	4	0	9	9	46^1	57	8	3.7	4.5	23	51%	.320
2016	NAS	AAA	26	1	7	0	15	15	66^2	72	4	4.6	6.2	46	55%	.318
2017	OAK	MLB	27	3	6	0	14	13	69^2	78	4	3.5	7.1	55	47%	.327
2017	NAS	AAA	27	2	0	0	6	5	25	28	1	5.0	6.5	18	54%	.342
2019	KCA	MLB	29	1	1	0	15	0	16	16	1	4.8	6.8	12	46%	.292

Breakout: 28%   Improve: 47%   Collapse: 24%   Attrition: 20%   MLB: 84%
Comparables: Roberto Hernandez, Jimmy Nelson, Randy Wells

A teammate of Matt Harvey's at Fitch Senior High School in Groton, Connecticut, Hahn has followed a career path with less fame and infamy than his former rotation partner. But the degree to which both righties have fallen on hard times and debilitating injuries makes you wonder if there was a late-night, disturbed-burial-ground prank that went wrong sometime back in the mid-aughts. The latest chapter in Hahn's book of misfortune: a wonky UCL that was fixed by a "primary repair" surgery—a non-Tommy John procedure requiring only six months of rehab. It's not exactly encouraging that the only other major-league pitcher to undergo this surgery, Seth Maness, enjoyed a mere 9 2/3 major-league innings (with the Royals!) before his release. For Hahn, a comeback of even that duration is beginning to feel like a positive outcome.

YEAR	TEAM	LVL	AGE	WHIP	ERA	DRA	WARP	MPH	FB%	WHF	CSP
2016	OAK	MLB	26	1.64	6.02	6.21	-0.5	96.4	71.9	6.5	48.9
2016	NAS	AAA	26	1.59	4.32	4.03	1.0				
2017	OAK	MLB	27	1.51	5.30	5.94	-0.3	95.9	61.8	8	49.7
2017	NAS	AAA	27	1.68	4.32	4.68	0.3				
2019	KCA	MLB	29	1.51	4.88	5.06	0.0	95.4	64.9	7.5	49.4

Richard Lovelady LHP

Born: 07/07/95 Age: 23 Bats: L Throws: L
Height: 6'0" Weight: 175 Origin: Round 10, 2016 Draft (#313 overall)

YEAR	TEAM	LVL	AGE	W	L	SV	G	GS	IP	H	HR	BB/9	K/9	K	GB%	BABIP
2016	ROY	RK	20	2	0	3	8	0	10^1	4	0	1.7	12.2	14	52%	.174
2016	IDA	RK	20	0	1	6	13	0	14^2	10	0	4.3	9.8	16	71%	.294
2017	WIL	A+	21	1	0	7	21	0	33^1	18	0	1.1	11.1	41	70%	.237
2017	NWA	AA	21	3	2	3	21	0	33^1	28	1	3.5	9.7	36	50%	.310
2018	OMA	AAA	22	3	3	9	46	0	73	53	3	2.6	8.8	71	51%	.262
2019	KCA	MLB	23	3	1	2	53	0	55^2	52	6	4.5	8.5	53	51%	.294

Breakout: 12% Improve: 22% Collapse: 20% Attrition: 28% MLB: 47%
Comparables: Corey Knebel, Eduardo Sanchez, Bruce Rondon

Like first-base prospects, minor-league pitchers already placed in the "reliever" bucket have gotten a bad rap. But after a Brewers playoff run that saw every broadcaster and analyst breathlessly obsess over Josh Hader whether or not he was actually pitching, future bullpen arms can now step into the light and puff their chests with pride over their newfound importance. Lovelady is vaguely Haderesque in his high-90s velocity and low-slung arm slot, and after a season that saw him emerge from the abattoir of the PCL relatively bloodlessly, he should have the chance to arrive in the majors in 2019. Whether he becomes a LOOGY, a multi-inning stopper, or a closer, the opportunities—and the puerile nicknames—should be plentiful.

YEAR	TEAM	LVL	AGE	WHIP	ERA	DRA	WARP	MPH	FB%	WHF	CSP
2016	ROY	RK	20	0.58	1.74	1.88	0.4				
2016	IDA	RK	20	1.16	1.84	3.76	0.3				
2017	WIL	A+	21	0.66	1.08	2.99	0.7				
2017	NWA	AA	21	1.23	2.16	3.68	0.4				
2018	OMA	AAA	22	1.01	2.47	2.45	2.2				
2019	KCA	MLB	23	1.43	4.55	4.77	0.3				

Daniel Lynch LHP

Born: 11/17/96 Age: 22 Bats: L Throws: L
Height: 6'6" Weight: 190 Origin: Round 1C, 2018 Draft (#34 overall)

YEAR	TEAM	LVL	AGE	W	L	SV	G	GS	IP	H	HR	BB/9	K/9	K	GB%	BABIP
2018	BNC	RK	21	0	0	0	3	3	11^1	9	0	1.6	11.1	14	59%	.310
2018	LEX	A	21	5	1	0	9	9	40	35	1	1.4	10.6	47	51%	.343
2019	KCA	MLB	22	2	3	0	8	8	34^2	35	4	3.2	8.3	32	45%	.314

Breakout: 4%   Improve: 7%   Collapse: 4%   Attrition: 7%   MLB: 12%
Comparables: Carson Fulmer, Nik Turley, Frankie Montas

After Florida's Brady Singer and Jackson Kowar, Lynch, a Virginia product, was the third piece of the big-college pitcher draft strategy for the Royals in 2018. While the race to the majors is long, even for advanced prospects such as these, Lynch jumped out to an early lead by breezing through rookie ball and logging a productive stretch at Low-A Lexington, where he displayed both turbo velocity and excellent control. Given his spotty secondary pitches and flying-bundle-of-sticks mechanics, the likeliest outcome for Lynch is as a power lefty out of the pen, which could put him on an even faster track to a major-league debut than the other members of his draft cohort.

YEAR	TEAM	LVL	AGE	WHIP	ERA	DRA	WARP	MPH	FB%	WHF	CSP
2018	BNC	RK	21	0.97	1.59	3.28	0.3				
2018	LEX	A	21	1.02	1.58	3.57	0.8				
2019	KCA	MLB	22	1.37	4.16	4.36	0.4				

Kansas City Royals 2019

Brady Singer   RHP
Born: 08/04/96   Age: 22   Bats: R   Throws: R
Height: 6'5"   Weight: 210   Origin: Round 1, 2018 Draft (#18 overall)

It might not have been "Old Man Yells at Cloud," but the widely-circulated video of the Royals' 2018 first-round pick spitting expletives at a College World Series delay might be titled "Young Man Curses at Rain." In spite of the extremely audible F-bombs, clean-livin' advocate Dayton Moore took this as a sign of Singer's competitive fire and evidence of that indefinable aura of "makeup." Intangibles aside, what is very tangible is Singer's talent and arsenal: a mid-90s fastball, complementary slider, and emerging changeup—all burnished in the elite competitive environment of the SEC. Once mentioned as a possible first-overall pick, Singer seemed to suffer from prospect fatigue despite winning a Dick Howser Award (for the best college player) and the SEC Pitcher of the Year Award. The Royals were apparently so happy to get him at pick 18 that they ended up going nearly a million dollars over slot to sign the righty. Challenging overused abbreviations addressing the ontology of pitching prospects, Singer will be expected to move quickly through the minors and arrive as a main rotation piece of the next competitive Royals team.

Josh Staumont RHP

Born: 12/21/93 Age: 25 Bats: R Throws: R
Height: 6'3" Weight: 200 Origin: Round 2, 2015 Draft (#64 overall)

YEAR	TEAM	LVL	AGE	W	L	SV	G	GS	IP	H	HR	BB/9	K/9	K	GB%	BABIP
2016	WIL	A+	22	2	10	0	18	15	73	62	3	8.3	11.6	94	46%	.328
2016	NWA	AA	22	2	1	0	11	11	50^1	42	2	6.6	13.1	73	42%	.364
2017	OMA	AAA	23	3	8	0	16	15	76	64	14	7.5	11.0	93	41%	.279
2017	NWA	AA	23	3	4	0	10	10	48^2	42	2	6.3	8.3	45	36%	.308
2018	OMA	AAA	24	2	5	1	41	5	74^1	59	4	6.3	12.5	103	44%	.327
2019	KCA	MLB	25	1	2	0	31	0	32	25	3	8.0	11.3	41	41%	.293

Breakout: 19% Improve: 24% Collapse: 9% Attrition: 26% MLB: 38%
Comparables: Esmerling Vasquez, Matt Magill, Kyle Crick

With his big, scary triple-digit fastball, Staumont stands out in a system in which command-control is the name of the game. Unfortunately, the fastball is, like, *really* scary, as no one in the park, much less Staumont himself, has any idea where it's going. It's a testament to his raw stuff that the power righty managed a Triple-A ERA that was little more than half of his BB/9. "Effectively wild" is often used as a backhanded compliment for a pitcher, but in Staumont's case, it's a life goal.

YEAR	TEAM	LVL	AGE	WHIP	ERA	DRA	WARP	MPH	FB%	WHF	CSP
2016	WIL	A+	22	1.77	5.05	4.10	1.1				
2016	NWA	AA	22	1.57	3.04	3.38	1.0				
2017	OMA	AAA	23	1.67	6.28	4.72	0.8				
2017	NWA	AA	23	1.56	4.44	4.74	0.2				
2018	OMA	AAA	24	1.49	3.51	3.77	1.2				
2019	KCA	MLB	25	1.66	4.77	4.96	0.1				

LINEOUTS

Hitters

HITTER	POS	TEAM	LVL	AGE	PA	R	2B	3B	HR	RBI	BB	K	SB	CS	AVG/OBP/SLG	DRC+	WARP
Gabriel Cancel	2B	WIL	A+	21	507	54	31	1	8	73	35	91	7	4	.259/.316/.385	100	0.4
Samir Duenez	1B	NWA	AA	22	328	44	18	2	10	60	35	68	5	0	.282/.357/.463	129	0.2
Kelvin Gutierrez	3B	HAR	AA	23	249	36	6	3	5	26	16	62	10	1	.274/.321/.391	96	1.8
	3B	NWA	AA	23	264	29	8	3	6	40	20	46	10	3	.277/.337/.409	104	0.4
Blake Perkins	CF	POT	A+	21	305	39	11	0	1	21	42	67	12	5	.234/.344/.290	101	0.0
	CF	WIL	A+	21	291	48	11	1	2	18	50	67	17	4	.240/.381/.322	100	1.6
Emmanuel Rivera	3B	WIL	A+	22	411	45	25	6	6	61	29	59	3	2	.280/.333/.427	109	0.0
Frank Schwindel	1B	OMA	AAA	26	556	65	38	1	24	93	34	71	2	2	.286/.336/.506	124	0.7
Bubba Starling	OF	OMA	AAA	25	41	5	2	0	0	2	5	6	1	0	.257/.350/.314	87	-0.1

In a full season as a 21 year-old in High-A, **Gabriel Cancel** started slow and finished strong, which is better than the opposite. With time on his side, and some room for growth in both power and speed, he may yet develop into a middle infielder who can offer more than bupkus with the bat. ⚾ If describing **Samir Duenez** as the second-best first-base prospect in an organization sounds like damnation by faint praise, well, at least his developing power and patience are praiseworthy. 2018 was not an ideal year to lose a half season to a wrist injury, as Duenez now has the promising Nick Pratto looming in the rear view mirror. ⚾ After an impressive 2017 that ended in Low-A Lexington, center field prospect **Michael Gigliotti** began 2018 with a pop—unfortunately, of his ACL. Given that Gigliotti's value resides with speed and defense—things you'd ideally want two healthy knees for—the clock is on pause until we see how he comes out of the gate in 2019. ⚾ In a rare Kelvin-for-Kelvin swap, the Royals received third baseman **Kelvin Gutierrez** from the Nationals when they shipped closer Herrera in a midseason deal. The current Kelvin is a capable defender who lacks the power one would prefer at a corner position, but even if he's rushed to the majors, his offensive production won't be an absolute zero. ⚾ **Blake Perkins** arrived in the Kelvin Herrera trade, providing the Royals another speedy centerfielder-type to their growing minor-league collection. Perkins stands out in this group for his patience at the plate and his switch-hitting, but if he makes it to the bigs, it will almost certainly be for defensive reasons. ⚾ Rare among Royals prospects for his advanced plate approach, **Emmanuel Rivera** is also a polished defender at the hot corner. While the big club has a desperate need for a third baseman, Rivera still needs some time in the oven, ideally to bake in more power. ⚾ After nearly a thousand Triple-A plate appearances with an .853 OPS and not even a sniff of the big club, the Royals seem to have decided that "King of Omaha" **Frank Schwindel** is organizational filler. The Royals will probably look elsewhere for a righty platoon partner for Ryan O'Hearn, but should they? ⚾ At this point, 2011 fifth-overall pick **Bubba Starling**, who lost last season to myriad injuries and has yet to see his major-league debut, would likely sell off parts of his soul to duplicate the five-win career of Bubba Trammell.

Pitchers

PITCHER	TEAM	LVL	AGE	W	L	SV	G	GS	IP	H	HR	BB/9	K/9	K	GB%	WHIP	ERA	DRA	WARP
Yefri Del Rosario	LEX	A	18	6	5	0	15	15	79	69	10	3.3	8.2	72	40%	1.24	3.19	4.95	0.2
Conner Greene	SFD	AA	23	4	3	0	11	10	48^2	43	1	5.9	8.0	43	49%	1.54	4.44	4.67	0.4
	MEM	AAA	23	0	2	0	29	0	39^1	33	2	7.1	5.9	26	47%	1.63	3.66	4.22	0.4
Foster Griffin	NWA	AA	22	10	12	0	28	26	152^2	197	20	2.4	6.9	117	39%	1.55	5.13	5.11	0.4
Carlos Hernandez	LEX	A	21	6	5	0	15	15	79^1	71	7	2.6	9.3	82	44%	1.18	3.29	6.02	-0.8
Tim Hill	KCA	MLB	28	1	4	2	70	0	45^2	46	4	2.8	8.3	42	64%	1.31	4.53	5.00	0.0
Jackson Kowar	LEX	A	21	0	1	0	9	9	26^1	19	2	4.1	7.5	22	59%	1.18	3.42	3.90	0.4
Ben Lively	PHI	MLB	26	0	2	0	5	5	23^2	34	4	3.8	8.4	22	30%	1.86	6.85	5.12	0.0
	LEH	AAA	26	3	2	0	11	8	52	37	3	2.6	8.1	47	43%	1.00	2.42	3.85	1.0
	KCA	MLB	26	0	1	0	5	0	6^2	7	0	6.8	6.8	5	55%	1.80	1.35	4.67	0.0
Andres Machado	OMA	AAA	25	0	4	0	7	6	25	41	4	5.8	9.0	25	51%	2.28	9.72	5.87	-0.1
	NWA	AA	25	2	3	9	30	6	58	60	5	3.4	7.3	47	45%	1.41	3.72	4.50	0.4
Jake Newberry	NWA	AA	23	2	0	12	25	0	29^2	29	2	2.4	11.2	37	32%	1.25	2.12	2.79	0.7
	OMA	AAA	23	3	0	3	16	0	20	13	1	2.7	7.2	16	51%	0.95	0.90	3.26	0.4
	KCA	MLB	23	2	0	0	14	0	13^1	13	3	6.1	7.4	11	32%	1.65	4.72	5.64	-0.1

Two things about **Yefri Del Rosario**: 1) He was an 18-year-old pitching in the Sally League. 2) He rejected better offers to sign with the Royals because of his respect for the late Yordano Ventura. His mid-90s fastball velocity is reminiscent of his idol, and he's got time on his side to develop his secondary offerings. ⚾ **Conner Greene** has a double consonant in one name, a double vowel in the other, flirts with triple digits on the fastball, and is doomed to a Quadruple A future in baseball. ⚾ The route from Arvest Ballpark in Springdale, Arkansas to Kauffman Stadium is pretty much a straight shot north on I-49—225 miles, according to Google Maps. With an underwhelming second year in Double-A, and a fastball that rarely touches 90 mph, **Foster Griffin** may as well measure that distance in light years. ⚾ Tall, slender, and projectable, **Carlos Hernandez** fared well in the better part of a season at Low-A. With an electric mid-90s sinker and (stop us if you've heard this before) still-developing secondary offerings, Hernandez has a future that falls in that Venn diagram intersection of "back-end starter" and "power reliever," which can be said of nearly every Royals pitching prospect not named Singer, Kowar, or Lynch. ⚾ **Tim Hill** shares a throwing side (left) and a last name with a certain pitcher who earned the nickname "Dick Mountain" from his Dodger teammates. Tim Hill can aspire to modest heights—Tim Rise, Tim Mound, Tim Butte, Tim Hummock—but he will never be Tim Mountain. ⚾ The Sundance Kid to Brady Singer's Butch Cassidy at the University of Florida, **Jackson Kowar** and his compadre will reprise their buddy-movie roles in the Royals system, having both been first-round picks of the club in 2018. Kowar has an angry fastball, but sometimes it shoots a little too straight, and rounding out the arsenal will be the primary quest for 2019. ⓧ The Royals claimed **Ben Lively** off of waivers from Philadelphia in September, because why not? The former prospect threw a handful of late-season innings out of the pen, jumping his four-seam velocity from the low- to mid-90s and possibly hinting at his future major-league role, if he is indeed to have one. ⓧ After a brief taste of the bigs in 2017, **Andres Machado** reversed course this past season. Demoted from Triple to Double-A in May and pushed into the bullpen shortly thereafter, the Venezuelan righty will need to re-discover his slider and his command before climbing back up the organizational ladder. ⓧ One instinctively roots for a 37th-round pick to make good, and if "making good" means pitching in the major leagues, then **Jake Newberry** realized a dream in August. Given a fringy fastball and middling secondary offerings, making a 25-man roster in 2019 might prove a second-level challenge.

Royals Prospects

The State of the System:
The Royals system is improving but still top-heavy. A loaded 2018 draft class could help the organization take the next step forward.

The Top Ten:

1. Seuly Matias   OF   OFP: 60   Likely: 50   ETA: 2022
Born: 09/04/98   Age: 20   Bats: R   Throws: R   Height: 6'3"   Weight: 200
Origin: International Free Agent, 2015

The Report: Scouts will often talk about how it "sounds different" when an elite prospect makes contact. Matias may not be an elite prospect yet, but it sounds like an M-80 when he squares one up. Not coincidentally, that's also the grade on his raw power projection. Matias has plus bat speed and gets easy extension. The power plays line-to-line when he connects—just ask Justus Sheffield—but he needs to make more contact. His swing isn't super stiff or overly leveraged and Matias' pitch recognition is pretty decent for a 19-year-old facing mostly older arms, but he swings hard and he'll come up empty fairly often. Lucky for him, a 35% strikeout rate isn't a deal breaker in today's game.

In the field Matias is an average runner at present and should be an average glove in a corner. He has plenty of arm for right, which is another plus-plus tool in his locker. He projects as your prototypical right field slugger. Matias may only hit .250, but it could come with a shiny OBP and 35 bombs.

The Risks: High. It's top of the scale power, but he will have to get most of it into games to carry the corner outfield profile and early returns on the hit tool are mixed.

Ben Carsley's Fantasy Take: This isn't my favorite profile for fantasy prospects, but it's hard not to drool when you hear about Matias' power potential. Assuming the rest of the profile holds up, Matias could end up as a slightly less prodigious version of Khris Davis, who was a top-15 outfielder in standard 5×5 formats this season. That being said, Matias could also end up going the Joey Gallo route, and that risk is enough to keep him from entering the upper echelon of dynasty outfield prospects. He's still a good one, though.

Kansas City Royals 2019

2. Khalil Lee OF
OFP: 60   Likely: 50   ETA: 2021
Born: 06/26/98   Age: 21   Bats: L   Throws: L   Height: 5'10"   Weight: 170
Origin: Round 3, 2016 Draft (#103 overall)

The Report: Overall, Lee is still raw at the plate, but he showed an advanced approach and strong feel for the strike zone while cutting down on his strikeouts in 2018. A 15.9% walk rate at High-A is nothing to scoff at, and though he struggled at Double-A, there's little question about his athleticism or ability to make adjustments. The raw power is above-average at present, and when he turns on a fastball, it's a sight to see.

Lee's lightning-fast hands allow him to get the bat through the zone quickly, and he's got plus bat speed and above-average control of the barrel. He should also be an above-average runner at full maturity. In center field, Lee is still learning. He'll take a bad route to a ball every now and again, but he fields his position competently. He'd be a plus defender at a corner spot, but there's plenty of time to let him develop up the middle. The tools are all there for Lee to be a productive player. His ultimate role will be shaped by how much of his power he can get to in games.

The Risks: High. There are times when Lee's mild bat wrap and short stride falls apart a bit at the plate, and the swing can get a little long when he rushes. If the above-average raw power doesn't show up in games, Lee's a solid table-setting top of the order guy. But if that power develops, you could see him in an All-Star Game or two.

Ben Carsley's Fantasy Take: I may be in the minority, but from a dynasty perspective I like Lee as the best prospect in this system. His speed is more valuable than Matias' power within the confines of fantasy, and I like his more well-rounded approach and multiple paths to value. I'm expecting to be the high guy on Lee all offseason, so take everything I'm saying here with a grain of salt, but he's already a borderline top-50 dynasty prospect for me.

3. MJ Melendez C
OFP: 60   Likely: 50   ETA: 2022
Born: 11/29/98   Age: 20   Bats: L   Throws: R   Height: 6'1"   Weight: 185
Origin: Round 2, 2017 Draft (#52 overall)

The Report: Melendez is fighting against 15 years of demographics. The last early-round prep catcher to turn into a reliable above-average regular was Brian McCann in 2002. "Catchers are weird" as we say around these parts, but we could also say "Prep catchers are usually first basemen." That's less of a concern with Melendez, who projects as an above-average defender due to his innate athleticism and plus throwing arm. The power is plus as well.

The lingering question with Melendez is that pesky ol' hit tool. His swing can get out of sync, and even when he's locked in there's length, loft, and issues with lefties. The bar for catcher offense is so low that even an Austin Hedgish bat would make Melendez a viable major leaguer, but there's still a lot of variance in the profile. That's normal for a 19-year-old prep catcher in the Sally, but it makes him risky enough to slot him third on this list, even if the ultimate ceiling here may be higher than the two outfielders ranked ahead of him.

The Risks: High. Prep catchers in A-ball are always going to check in at the upper end of our risk range, and Melendez has additional questions about how the hit tool will play at upper levels.

Ben Carsley's Fantasy Take: Melendez may be a good fantasy catching prospect, but fantasy catching prospects stink. Given the long lead time, the risk and the good-but-not-great Wilson Ramos-esque ceiling here, Melendez is a prospect I'm likely going to lose out on to people who value the position more. At this point I think the attrition rate for catchers is just too high to put them on the top-101, but we'll see how I feel once I've written up 300-plus other guys.

4 — Brady Singer   RHP
OFP: 60   Likely: 50   ETA: 2020
Born: 08/04/96   Age: 22   Bats: R   Throws: R   Height: 6'5"   Weight: 210
Origin: Round 1, 2018 Draft (#18 overall)

The Report: The Royals leveraged the largest draft pool in the league to go nearly a million over slot to nab Singer, who tumbled on draft day due to his bonus demands. The Gators Friday night starter dominated the SEC on the strength of his plus fastball/slider combo. The fastball reaches the mid-90s, and the slider shows hard, late tilt. But there is more reliever risk here then you'd expect/hope for from the second-best college arm in the draft. Singer's slot is a tick below three-quarters, and there is significant effort in his arm action. His changeup needs refinement to give him an armside weapon against lefties given the lower slot, and the Royals might be best off letting him air it out in 1-2 inning bursts. Ultimately, we have here a classic mid-rotation starter or late-inning reliever profile.

The Risks: Medium. No pro track record to speak of—although you could argue Friday night starter in the SEC is basically A-ball—and there's legitimate relief risk.

Ben Carsley's Fantasy Take: Singer is likely to be overvalued in dynasty drafts this offseason, as his draft slot/name recognition/SEC track record are going to fool some into thinking he's a potential future ace. He's not, and between the reliever risk and the fact that his ceiling appears to be something of a fantasy SP4/5, Singer should be valued as more of a fringe top-101 guy than a true fantasy stud in the making.

5 — Jackson Kowar   RHP
OFP: 55   Likely: 50   ETA: 2020
Born: 10/04/96   Age: 22   Bats: R   Throws: R   Height: 6'5"   Weight: 180
Origin: Round 1C, 2018 Draft (#33 overall)

The Report: As usual, the Florida Gators rotation was an embarrassment of prospect riches, and Kowar joined his college teammate in the Royals system after getting popped in the Comp A round. Kowar doesn't have Singer's raw stuff, but his delivery looks the part of a major-league starter and his mid-90s fastball is nothing to sneeze at. The big heater showed up less in his first pro summer—sitting more 93-94 in A-ball—and it can run a bit true, but Kowar shows above-average command of the pitch. A pitcher's first professional summer can be a tricky time to evaluate them, though some guys never throw harder than they did in college. If the consistent plus velocity comes back, it will round out an arsenal with two potential above-average secondaries. Kowar's changeup is more advanced at present, while his power curveball requires a bit more projection. Right now, its shape is inconsistent but flashes plus with hard biting action.

The Risks: Medium. Obviously there isn't much professional track record, and also less swing-and-miss stuff than you'd like from a highly-ranked college arm. But Kowar is fairly polished and he should encounter few speed bumps in the minors beyond the usual pitcher health concerns.

Ben Carsley's Fantasy Take: Kowar may be a safer bet to return at least *some* fantasy value than Singer is, but ultimately he's shaping up to be a pretty replaceable fantasy asset. He might be worthy of a stash once he's closer to the majors, but you can keep the dime-a-dozen back-end starter prospects on waivers when they're this far from the show.

6. Nicky Lopez IF OFP: 55 Likely: 45 ETA: 2019
Born: 03/13/95 Age: 24 Bats: L Throws: R Height: 5'11" Weight: 175
Origin: Round 5, 2016 Draft (#163 overall)

The Report: Fans of The Grinder—the short-lived Fred Savage/Rob Lowe FOX comedy vehicle—take heart: Nicky Lopez may be coming to a baseball park near you in time for the 2019 upfronts. Is he actually 5-foot-11? Probably not. Can he really play shortstop? He'll give you all he's got. Is he a pest at the plate? You betcha. He'll choke up, foul off, and draw walks. He's a fringy runner, but he'll grab the extra base where he can. He's short to the ball, contact-oriented, and his uniform is gonna be dirty by the time the mascot race rolls around. This profile is always tricky, because it lacks a carrying tool, and a well-below-average power projection means that major-league pitchers are going to be able to challenge him. Lopez will have to prove he can hit at every level, but at least now there is only one level left to go.

The Risks: Medium. You could call Lopez low risk given his approach, bat control, and defensive flexibility, but sometimes these profiles get the bat knocked out of their hands at the highest level.

Ben Carsley's Fantasy Take: With all due respect to Brock Holt, do you really want to roster the prospect version of Brock Holt?

7 | **Nick Pratto   1B** | OFP: 55   Likely: 45   ETA: 2021
Born: 10/06/98   Age: 20   Bats: L   Throws: L   Height: 6'1"   Weight: 195
Origin: Round 1, 2017 Draft (#14 overall)

The Report: Pratto does not have your typical first-base profile. Most first-base prospects are big, power-first bats playing other positions in the minor leagues. Pratto breaks that mold a bit as an undersized hit-first lefty. His hit tool is the most impressive of the bunch, but he was able to tap into a bit of power this season. While he doesn't have prototypical first-base size, Pratto is strong throughout, with plenty of wrist and forearm strength. He may never hit 30 bombs in a season, but you can expect plenty of doubles.

Pratto has an advanced approach. He rarely has bad at-bats and sees the ball really well. He's balanced at the plate, and his quick hips let him get to velocity and anything on the inner-half. Pratto is also capable of hitting the ball to all fields. No one is going to call him "fast" but you can expect healthy steal totals from a really smart, Goldschmidt-esque runner. He should also wind up one of the better defenders at his position. You won't get to see it often, but Pratto throws well, and some considered him a two-way prospect as an amateur

The Risks: High. There is no room for error when it comes to first basemen. If the bat don't play, you don't play.

Ben Carsley's Fantasy Take: You need to be a really good hitter or really potent slugger to be a worthwhile fantasy first baseman. Guys who sort of fall just short of either distinction—your Yonder Alonsos, Brandon Belts, and Eric Hosmers, etc—generally end up ranking somewhere between the 20th and 35th best options at the position. That's what we're likely going to see from Pratto, which makes him worth rostering in deep leagues and an afterthought in shallower formats.

8 | **Daniel Lynch   LHP** | OFP: 55   Likely: 45
ETA: As a reliever in 2019. 2020 is more likely.
Born: 11/17/96   Age: 22   Bats: L   Throws: L   Height: 6'6"   Weight: 190
Origin: Round 1C, 2018 Draft (#34 overall)

The Report: The pre-draft reports all had Lynch as a projectable lefty currently pinned around 90 mph. Well, in a bit of TV cooking show magic, the rib roast goes in the oven and one clock wipe later he's touching 97 in the pros. The velocity range is still wide here, but Lynch will sit 93-95 with good boring action in on righties. He's able to reach back for plus-plus velo late in outings and he elevates the pitch effectively.

The secondaries are more forgettable side dishes at present. Lynch's slider can flatten out, and he struggles to get it down in the zone consistently, but it flashes 55 with big tilt. The breaking ball also comes in from a tough angle for fellow lefties. The change doesn't always turnover for him, and it can be too firm, but he'll show a hard sinking version at times that bumps average. There should be enough cambio for him to crossover at least.

The mechanics might force him to the pen, as it's a slingy arm action thrown across his body with some effort. Control is well ahead of command at present, and he'll have tall pitcher issues with regard to repeating his delivery. It's not quite "set it, and forget it" yet, but Lynch won't need sous vide cooking times to impact the majors.

The Risks: Medium. Lynch dominated levels you'd expect him too, and the command issues won't come to a head until the upper minors, but as a lefty with a plus fastball, a decent slider, and some funk, there's a major-league role here, health permitting.

Ben Carsley's Fantasy Take: How many non-closing relievers were rostered in your league last year? Yeah...

9 Kris Bubic   LHP   OFP: 50   Likely: 40   ETA: 2021
Born: 08/19/97   Age: 21   Bats: L   Throws: L   Height: 6'3"   Weight: 220
Origin: Round 1, 2018 Draft (#40 overall)

The Report: Hey, it's another polished lefty with a deceptive delivery and a potential plus changeup! Bubic was a dominant starter for Stanford this past spring on the strength of his change and he continued to miss bats with it in the pros. He sells the pitch well, and while it doesn't feature huge fade, the 10-15 mph gap between the cambio and his fastball gets guys to swing through, Bugs Bunny-style. The fastball can sit in the low-90s, but sometimes only touches 90. He still gets late swings on it due to his hitchy, uphill delivery and some gloveside run.

Bubic's unorthodox mechanics tend to impact his control and command of the fastball though. His path can wander during his long arm action, and he doesn't always get on top of his release. There's a tradeoff here obviously, but it remains to be seen if he can throw enough quality strikes with the fastball at the upper levels to set up his change. The breaking ball is a slurvy curveball that flashes average, but is even more inconsistent than Kowar's. It's fine as a show-me pitch to lefties, but lacks the depth to be a bat-misser at present. Bubic has a mature frame with a thick lower half, so while he lacks physical projection, it's also a starting-pitching-ready body. His upside as a starter is limited though, without command or breaking ball improvement.

The Risks: Medium. Bubic is polished enough that he should breeze through the minors, but lefties with fringy heaters and breaking balls often bump the ceiling hard in the majors.

Ben Carsley's Fantasy Take: Too far away and too low a ceiling. No thank you.

10 **Kyle Isbel** **OF** OFP: 50   Likely: 40   ETA: 2021
Born: 03/03/97   Age: 22   Bats: L   Throws: R   Height: 5'11"   Weight: 183
Origin: Round 3, 2018 Draft (#94 overall)

The Report: Isbel is a smart player who will earn the "gritty" label soon enough. As you might expect, he plays hard, looks the part, and takes a patient approach at the dish. Isbel's quick hands cover the inner-half of the plate well, though his swing can lengthen at times. The power may end up a tick below average, but four tools could get to 50, and he's a plus runner. Isbel can handle center field and would be an above average defender in either corner spot. He played some infield at UNLV and there may be a world where Kansas City turns him into a utility type.

The Risks: Medium. Isbel will likely be worthy of an MLB roster spot, but if the bat doesn't develop, it's impossible to see an everyday or even a platoon role.

Ben Carsley's Fantasy Take: Isbel's speed could make him somewhat interesting if he finds himself with regular playing time, but the upside here is very, very modest. You don't need to pay attention until he's on an MLB roster.

The Next Five:

11 **Carlos Hernandez** **RHP**
Born: 03/11/97   Age: 22   Bats: R   Throws: R   Height: 6'4"   Weight: 175
Origin: International Free Agent, 2014

Hernandez was signed at 19, which is practically AARP age for international free agents. Usually when one of these guys hits, you've managed to find a polished arm who had a late-teenage velocity jump. Usually you pencil these guys in as relievers long term, but Hernandez has major-league starter upside. He's certainly got the frame, as he looks to be significantly heavier than his listed 175, and his delivery doesn't have any notable red flags. While his fastball works in an average velo band (91-94) he can show more in short bursts, and he commands the pitch well to both sides. There is some giddy up when he tries to elevate for strikeouts as well.

Hernandez's breaker is a bit of a slurve. It can get humpy when he wants to drop it in, but there's a tighter 11-5 version which he can start in the zone and get chases or spot gloveside. The change is the clear third pitch, and Hernandez lacks consistent feel for it at present. If the breaking ball and change improve he'll project as a fourth starter although, sure, you could pencil him in as a reliever long-term.

12 **Kelvin Gutierrez** **3B**
Born: 08/28/94   Age: 24   Bats: R   Throws: R   Height: 6'3"   Weight: 215
Origin: International Free Agent, 2013

The glove-first third base profile will not be the most exciting one we'll catalog across our other 29 lists, but catalog it we shall. Gutierrez moves well at third, and he has good instincts and hands. He has an accurate plus-plus arm and projects as an above-average defender at the hot corner. He struggles with right-on-right spin, but will flash acceptable power, even if he sometimes elongates his swing to tap into it. Overall his swing plane is fairly flat, and Gutierrez sees the ball much better from lefties, making a short-side platoon outcome a distinct possibility. If he manages to show an average hit tool and fringy game power in the majors, the glove will be enough to support a fringe everyday role. Look, we warned you it wasn't that exciting.

13 Yefri Del Rosario   RHP
Born: 09/23/99   Age: 19   Bats: R   Throws: R   Height: 6'2"   Weight: 180
Origin: International Free Agent, 2017

del Rosario grew up idolizing Yordano Ventura. There are reports on the kids of Mike Cameron, Vlad Guerrero, and Fernando Tatis elsewhere in this publication, but that is the sentence that's made me feel the oldest so far in this gig. Anywho, it shouldn't be a huge surprise then that del Rosario signed with the Royals after being granted free agency as part of the punishment for the Braves CBA violations in Latin America. Unlike his idol though, del Rosario isn't particularly likely to stick in a major-league rotation. There's some projection left in his 6-foot-2 frame, and I'd expect him to sit more consistently in the mid-90s as he matures (he works more in the low-90s now, although he'll touch 95 or higher). The fastball is a lively pitch with some natural cut, and del Rosario pairs it with a very projectable curveball for an 18-year-old. The velocity and shape can be wildly inconsistent, but he'll show a tight downer in the upper-70s. The change is firm, but occasionally flashes split action.

While del Rosario might develop three pitches in time, his mechanics may limit him to the pen. It's arm speed and torque over leg drive, and his halves tend to get out of sync. The arm action requires some effort as well, and while he generally throws strikes, he tends to be wild within the zone. del Rosario is athletic enough to keep it all mostly together, but if you need to project two pitches and a command jump, you can usually also project a move to the bullpen.

14 Blake Perkins   OF
Born: 09/10/96   Age: 22   Bats: B   Throws: R   Height: 6'1"   Weight: 165
Origin: Round 2, 2015 Draft (#69 overall)

Part of the Kelvin Herrera trade in June, the switch-hitting Perkins ended up being That Guy You Saw Too Much Of. And that's certainly not a bad thing; Perkins could become a fun player to watch at the top of a lineup. As the year went on, there was a bit more fight in his bat, and he'd work the count well enough and draw walks. But he doesn't hit for much power, and he's often trying to go the other way and slap a ball through the infield. He also seems much more comfortable from the right side of the plate at the moment. Defensively, he can handle center field: He's a sound route runner, and he'll wow you with his ability to reach balls in the gaps. His arm isn't much to write home about, but his instincts make him a sure bet to stick in center.

15 Meibrys Viloria C
Born: 02/15/97   Age: 22   Bats: L   Throws: R   Height: 5'11"   Weight: 220
Origin: International Free Agent, 2013

Viloria might have been the most unlikely big-league call-up this past season. With his year winding down with High-A Wilmington, Viloria was expected to wrap things up and get a break before heading to the AFL. Surprise! Injuries and a roster shuffle pushed Viloria from Wilmington all the way to Kansas City in September, and his advanced approach at the plate and arm prevented him from looking too helpless out there. He posted pop times around 1.93-1.95 and he's got an accurate arm, but he still needs a lot of work behind the plate. He doesn't have the softest hands, and he'll clank a few balls here and there. As he fills out, he could develop into a 15-homer guy and average game-caller with a plus arm. But first, a return to the minors awaits.

Others of note:

Daniel Tillo, LHP, High-A Wilmingon

Another large lefty in a system full of sizeable southpaws, the 6-foot-5 Tillo doesn't have Lynch's fastball or Bubic's change, but his tall-and-fall delivery and slingy, three-quarters slot makes for a tough AB for same-side sluggers. The fastball comes in around 90, but it offers solid plane and bores in on righties. Tillo will guide the change a bit, but there's good sink at times, and he is comfortable throwing it behind in counts. He also mixes in a short slider as well. The results weren't great for a 22-year-old college arm in A-ball, but there's enough rawness left that you can dream on a bit of projection being left in the profile. Barring that, you can always wring a LOOGY out of this.

Josh Staumont, RHP, Triple-A Omaha

Richard Lovelady, LHP, Triple-A Omaha

Two relief prospects coming from opposite ends of Royals prospect lists and meeting in Others of Note in 2019.

Staumont finally got his long-assumed conversion to relief in 2018. But there wasn't much room for the stuff to bump, and he still struggled to throw strikes in shorter bursts. As many bats as his power fastball/curve combo may miss when he's running good, he'll issue almost as many walks. The culprit is still an uptempo—bordering on violent—delivery, combined with a long arm action to get to his overhand slot. The over the top angle makes his stuff even harder to square, but until he proves he can be more effectively wild—or preferably just less wild—it's hard to see a late inning major-league pen role in the near-term. He'll get chances though; guys with high-90s heat and a curve that flashes plus-plus always will. And hey, it kept him in the top ten a year longer than it maybe should have.

Richard Lovelady first came to wider prominence due to an... unfortunate bit of character saving on twitter dot com. But he also has power stuff, and he commands it far better than Staumont at present. Lovelady's fastball is a couple ticks shy of Staumont's but he changes levels well, and it also comes from a tricky angle due to his crossfire delivery and low-three-quarters slot. He pairs it with a plus slider that shows good, late depth. He's been a next ten stalwart for two years running now, but may make an impact in the Royals bullpen before Staumont. Lovelady may not have the same upside, but you don't have to wishcast nearly as much to see a lefty setup arm here.

Michael Gigliotti, OF, Low-A Lexington

Gigliotti rounded out our top ten last year, but a knee injury ended his 2018 season after just a week. An ACL issue is not what you want for any prospect, but it will have an even more profound effect on Gigliotti, who generates much of his value from his plus-plus speed in center field. Until we see him back on the field and running down balls in the gap with similar aplomb, he's back to sleeperdom in an improving Royals system.

Top Talents 25 and Under (born 4/1/93 or later):

1. Adalberto Mondesi
2. Seuly Matias
3. Khalil Lee
4. MJ Melendez
5. Brady Singer
6. Jackson Kowar
7. Brad Keller
8. Ryan O'Hearn
9. Brett Phillips
10. Nicky Lopez

Last year's edition of this list was (let's be honest) really, really bad. This year's list is still bad but at least it's interesting bad—and that may be the first sign that Dayton Moore is slowly beginning to turn the creaking frame of the organizational ship toward the friendlier waters of a legitimate rebuild.

Same person, different name: last year's #1 Raul has become this year's #1 Adalberto. But after a superlative late-season run, a straight ordinal ranking cannot capture the distance between Mondesi and numbers two through ten on this list. The power production arrived unexpectedly while he fully actualized his speed at the major-league level. All that being said, a sober assessment has to note that the breakout came in both a small sample and with a continuation of some worrying peripherals, most obviously his aversion to taking walks (3.8 BB%), which, barring a significant change of approach, hard-caps his on-base potential around .300. Additionally, with a 19.7 HR/FB% almost certain to regress, you'd be optimistic to expect more than 15-20 homers in a full season. None of this cold water means Mondesi isn't a talent: Even if his approach might make for a bumpy ride, the defense is strong, and the speed is elite. It all makes for a package that is immensely fun to watch.

After the great tranche of prospects come two out-of-the blue major-league producers from 2018. Well, the second half of 2018, anyway. Keller, a Rule 5 pick from the Diamondbacks in 2017, was the most consistent Royals starter all season (something something land of the blind, one-eyed man, king). Even looking charitably at a strong final two months, where he cut his walks and started missing a few bats, Keller is a fairly standard-issue pitch-to-contact groundballer, which tightens the upside-floor bar between a No. 3 and No. 4 starter. Just behind Keller lies O'Hearn, who displayed a sudden power spike that only seems bizarre these days because the lefty-hitting first baseman didn't alter his swing plane at all. O'Hearn was slugging .391 in 406 PA at Triple-A before shredding major-league arms to the tune of a .262/.353/.597 line over the final two months. His exit velocities suggest legit power, and he also brings double-digit walk rates, but he was helpless against lefties after his call-up. Suffice to say, there's a sizable scoop of interest here, but it comes dolloped with heaping toppings of uncertainty.

Phillips, the major piece in the Mike Moustakas trade, earns a back-end spot over fellow outfielder Jorge Bonifacio based on the fact that he has the defensive chops for centerfield (oh, that right arm!) and hopes of developing an offensive profile that could yield everyday work. Bonifacio, by contrast, had a league-average 422 major-league plate appearances, got slapped with an 80-game PED suspension, then came back to have 270 below-average plate appearances. In particular, the disappearance of his power bodes poorly. If you've got a ceiling of an everyday centerfielder with league-average offense and a corner outfielder who will likely impress with neither on-base nor power abilities, you take the former all day, every day (even if it means more airtime for his inimitable donkey-pterodactyl laugh).

Kansas City Royals 2019

Even if it isn't yet reflected in this list, the Royals—aided significantly by the infusion of college pitching arms at the top of the draft—are beginning those slow, painful steps toward a rebuild. There's not much short-term hope at the major-league level, but at least the pipeline has something more than rust, cobwebs, and the musty stench of despair in it.

Part 3: Featured Articles

The Hole in The Shift is Fixing Itself

Russell Carleton

I've been on a bit of a mission against The Shift of late. I'm not out to get The Shift for the usual reasons that people oppose it. The words "the right way to play the game" won't be found on my lips. If a team wants to pursue a strategy that is within the rules and it works, then by all means, they have my blessing (not that they need it). Instead, my concern with The Shift is a worry that it doesn't work, or at least that it has a flaw that needs fixing.

The data show that while The Shift does a decent job of preventing singles on balls in play (what it's supposed to do), it also increases the number of walks that happen in front of it, and the number of additional walks outweighs the number of singles saved. It's a problem because you can't throw a guy out if he gets to walk to first base.

But the "why" was important. It seemed that The Shift was changing the way in which pitchers pitched. We saw that there were fewer fastballs thrown in front of The Shift than we might otherwise expect, and that pitchers tended to stay out of the strike zone a little more. Not by a lot. In fact, it might not even be visible to the naked eye. The percentage of pitches that are out of the zone goes from 51.0 to 53.3 from a standard defense (two right/two left) to a full shift (three on one side). That difference stands up even after we control for the types of hitters that get shifted against. And it's enough to drive up the walk rate to where it cancels out the benefits that teams thought they were getting with The Shift… and then some.

But there was some hope. I found that when individual pitchers stayed closer to the in-zone/out-of-zone mix that they used without The Shift on, they could still get the benefits of The Shift without the walk problems. So, in theory, a team could simply figure out a way to convince its pitchers to not fall prey to the walk trap and The Shift would once again be their friend.

It's reasonable to think that some teams might be more hip to this idea than others. Maybe some figured it out a year before the others. Maybe they were better at getting the message across to their pitchers. Or, maybe no one has figured it out yet.

Warning! Gory Mathematical Details Ahead!

I used data from 2015-2017, made available through MLB's data portal, Baseball Savant. They are kind enough to note when teams are using an infield shift (three fielders on one side of second base), as opposed to a "strategic shift" (someone's playing a bit out of position, but it's not quite that drastic) or a "standard" alignment.

Since we're doing this by team, I can't just look at raw walk rates, because we know that some teams have good pitchers and others have not-so-good pitchers. Some have a mix of both. I used the log-odds ratio method to take into account a batter's general walking proclivities, and a pitcher's as well, and then shoving them into a binary logistic regression. Then, I asked the computer to generate a specific coefficient for each team's pitchers, for when they went into The Shift and how that affected their walk rate.

Using those coefficients, I was able to project what would happen if a league-average pitcher faced a league-average hitter (which we expect would produce a league-average walk rate; from 2015-2017, 7.7 percent of plate appearances ended in a walk) and then just switched his hat. Here's the top five and the bottom five:

Top 5 Teams	Projected Shift Walk Rate	Bottom 5 Teams	Projected Shift Walk Rate
Rockies	6.2%	Rangers	11.2%
Pirates	6.7%	Mets	10.4%
Indians	7.2%	Dodgers	10.2%
Astros	7.3%	Cardinals	9.9%
Braves	7.7%	Tigers	9.7%

There are probably people out there right now trying to figure out what the common thread is among the top and bottom teams. I'm sure, because this is Baseball Prospectus, people are already trying to make the case that sabermetric "early adopters" have some sort of edge here. I think that the more interesting piece is that by the time you get to fifth place in The Shift, we're at league average.

As a sanity check, I examined the issue on a pitch-by-pitch level, looking at how often pitchers threw their pitches in the GameDay strike zone, and again using the same basic methodology and getting team-specific coefficients. The names on the list re-arranged themselves, but the idea was the same, and the two lists correlated with an R of .593.

There's a reason that I don't usually do this type of leaderboard post. I don't really know what the Rockies, Pirates, Indians, Astros, and Braves have in common, or what they have that the bottom five don't. I can put a shrug emoji here and say, "Well, it must be something!" but that seems like a cop-out. Instead, I'd like to present another table and suggest that the table above doesn't even really matter anymore.

Year	League Percent Outside K Zone (Full Shift)	League Percent in K Zone (No Shift)	Difference
2015	54.1%	51.1%	3.0%
2016	53.3%	50.9%	2.4%
2017	52.6%	50.9%	1.7%
2018	52.0%	50.7%	1.3%

The hole in The Shift is fixing itself, and it's coming down really fast league wide. In my earlier work on The Shift, I suggested that until teams stopped having such a huge difference between their out-of-zone rate with and without The Shift on, there would just be too many walks for The Shift to make sense. It seems that all 30 of them have been working toward just that. I once estimated that it takes about 10 years for an idea to filter its way through baseball. At this rate, it looks like teams are going to catch up a lot faster than that. And yeah, they're all saber-smart now.

It's likely that whatever magic it was that the Rockies and Pirates had has made its way to Texas and Queens. Or is at least on its way. And if teams are committing to fixing the walk problem, then it's likely that they will continue shifting and shifting a lot.

And eventually it's going to actually make sense for them to do it.

—*Russell Carleton is a former author of Baseball Prospectus and now an analyst for the New York Mets.*

The State of the Quality Start

Rob Mains

One of the seven things you (probably) didn't know about the 2018 season is that quality starts—defined as a start lasting six or more innings with three or fewer earned runs allowed—as a percentage of total starts cratered to an all-time low of 41 percent. I want to look a little more deeply into this, since it's been a while (May of 2016, to be exact) since I've examined quality starts.

The term *quality start* is credited to *Philadelphia Inquirer* sportswriter John Lowe. It's been derided ever since he coined it in December of 1985. Three runs in six innings? That's a 4.50 ERA! In what world is that a measure of quality?

Let's start with that criticism. It's true that 3 x 9 / 6 = 4.5. (You came here for this sort of high-level math, right?) But it's also true that type of start, meeting the bare minimum for earning a quality start, is unusual. Here's the proportion of quality starts in which the pitcher lasted exactly six innings and yielded exactly three earned runs. (I'm going to confine this analysis to the 30-team era, 1998-present. Almost all data retrieved in this article is via the Baseball-Reference Play Index.)

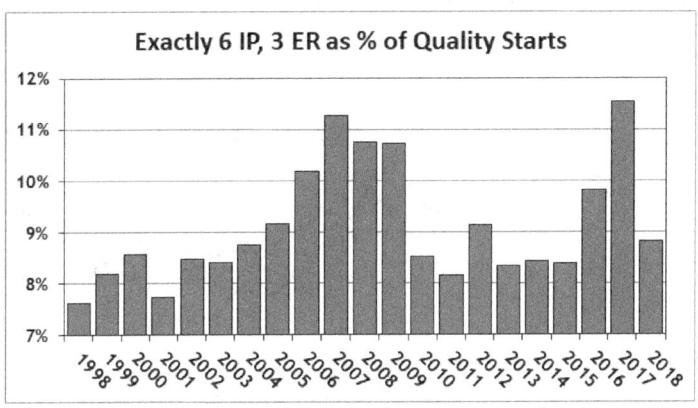

There were 1,997 quality starts in 2018. Only 176, or fewer than one in 11, featured a pitcher going six innings and allowing three earned runs. Put another way, the percentage of quality starts that resulted in a 4.50 ERA (8.8 percent) is less than half the percentage of games in which a batter hit two home runs and his team lost (22.5 percent; 237-69 won-lost). That doesn't impugn hitting two homers.

So if a 4.50 ERA isn't the norm, what is? How good are quality starts? Pretty good, it turns out. First, on a team level:

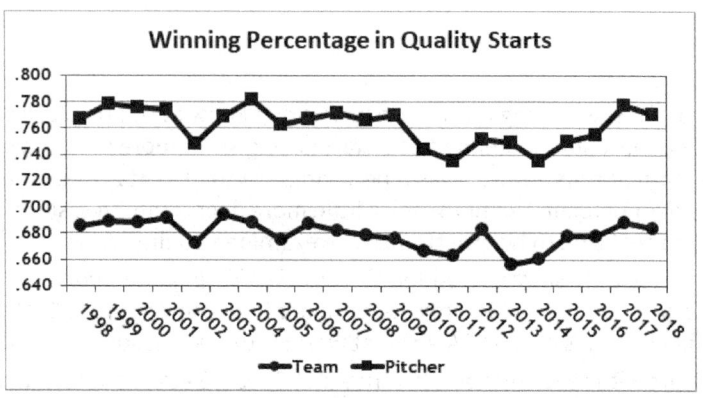

Teams receiving a quality start from their pitcher won 68.4 percent of their games in 2018, in line with the 30-team era average of 67.9 percent. A team with a .684 winning percentage wins 111 games. Getting a quality start is definitely a good thing. Individual pitchers throwing quality starts have a higher winning percentage because a big slice of team losses is assigned to a reliever.

If teams do well in quality starts, how well do the starting pitchers do? Again, very well.

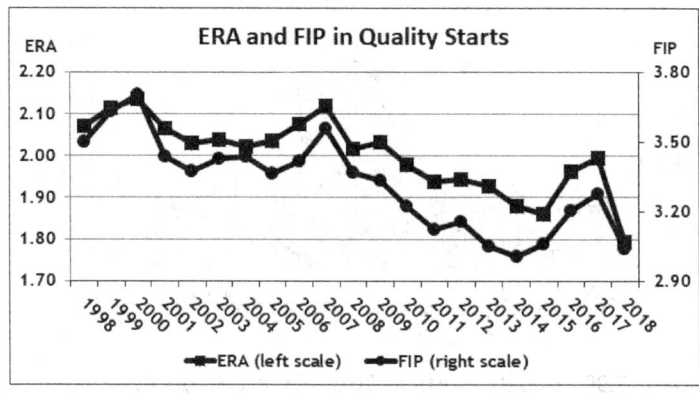

Pitchers in quality starts had a 1.79 ERA (blue line) in 2018, *the lowest in the 30-team era*. Their FIP was higher, 3.04, but still excellent. In the 30-team era, only 2014 had a lower FIP for quality starts, 3.01.

But, of course, the run environment in 2014 was different. Teams in 2014 scored 4.07 runs per game, the fewest in a non-strike year since 1976. They scored 4.45 runs per game in 2018. So surrendering a 3.04 FIP in 2018 is more impressive than 3.01 in 2014. Accordingly, let's look at ERA and FIP in quality starts relative to league averages.

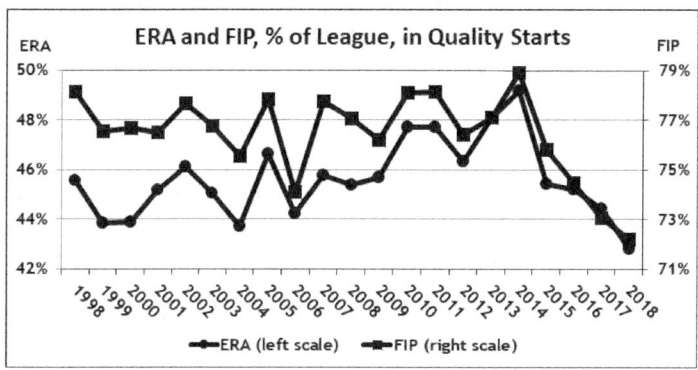

This tells a more dramatic story. Starting pitchers in 2018 gave up a 4.19 ERA and a 4.21 FIP. Starters in quality starts gave up a 1.79 ERA, 43 percent of the league average. Starters in quality starts gave up a 3.04 FIP, 72 percent of the league average. Both of these marks represent lows in the 30-team era.

The takeaway here is this: *Quality starts are better, relative to other starts, than they've ever been over the past 21 years.*

Maybe during the winter I'll look at this over a longer arc of time. For now, though, we can definitively say quality starts are the best they've ever been since the Diamondbacks and Rays joined the majors.

Yet, paradoxically, they're down.

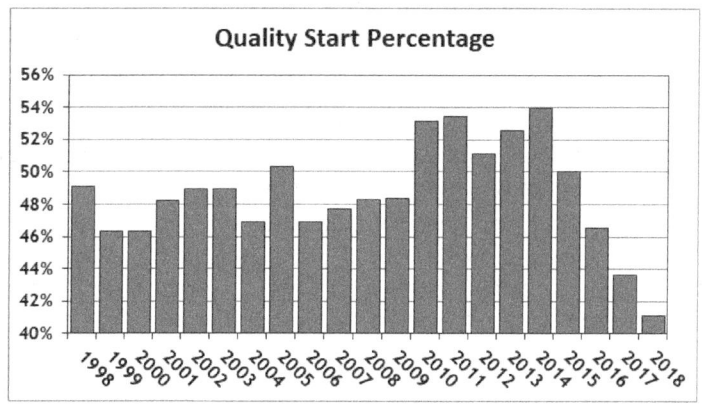

This graph covers only the 30-team era. In my article last week, though, I looked at the years 1908-2018. The result was the same. The 41 percent of starts in 2018 that were quality starts are an all-time low, well below the runners-up: 1930's 43 percent (the year teams scored an all-time record 5.55 runs per game) and last year's 44 percent.

The normal explanation for a dip in quality start percentage is an increase in scoring. When teams score a lot of runs, it's harder for starting pitchers to last six or more innings and limit opponents to three earned runs. From 1998 to 2014, the correlation between runs scored per game and the percentage of starts that were quality starts was -0.94. That means there was an extremely close relationship: More runs, fewer quality starts. Too small a sample? Go back to the start of the Expansion Era, 1961, and the relationship is even more negative, a -0.95 correlation, though 2014.

But that's broken down over the past four years:

- 2015: Runs per game increased from 4.07 to 4.25, quality start percentage decreased from 54.0 to 50.1. Yes, that's a negative relationship, but the regression model would predict a decline of 1.5 percentage points. We got 3.9 instead.
- 2016: Runs per game increased from 4.25 to 4.48, quality start percentage decreased from 50.1 to 46.6. Past experience would suggest a decline of just 1.8 percentage points. We got 3.4.
- 2017: Runs per game increased from 4.48 to 4.65, quality start percentage decreased from 46.6 to 43.6. Again, the direction's right, but the magnitude isn't. Using the relationship from 1998 to 2014, that increase in scoring should've reduced quality starts by 1.3 percentage points, not 2.9.
- 2018: Runs per game declined from 4.65 to 4.45. That should've resulted in the quality start percentage moving in the other direction, rising 1.6 points. It didn't. It fell 2.6 points, as noted, to an all-time low.

Granted, we're talking about just four years here. Maybe they're outliers. But I don't think they are. Quality starts, as noted, are as good or better than ever. But they're rarer than ever as well. And I think I know why.

To get a quality start, you need to allow three or fewer earned and pitch at least six innings. That's 18 outs. Here's a graph showing the number of starting pitchers who limited their opponents to three or fewer earned runs but got pulled after pitching at least five innings but fewer than six:

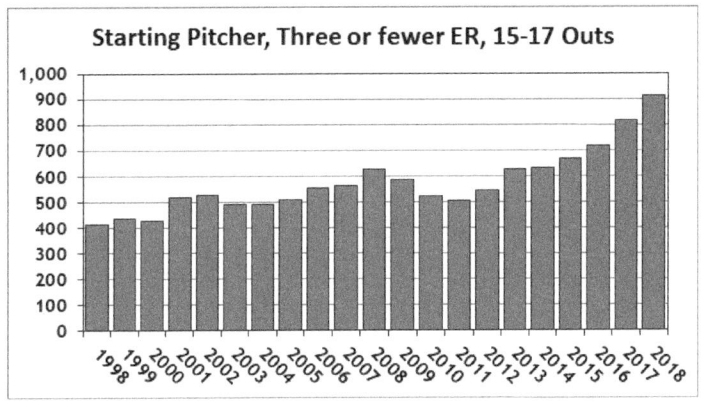

A pitcher getting 15 outs pitched five innings. A pitcher getting 16 outs pitched 5 1/3. A pitcher getting 17 outs pitched 5 2/3. More than ever before, pitchers are being removed from games in which they are within 1-3 outs of a quality start, falling just short of the six-inning finish line. Widespread acknowledgement of the times-through-the-order penalty and a flotilla of available bullpen arms is making the quality start simultaneously both more excellent and more rare.

Which is ironic, given that we saw a new post-war quality start record this season:

Rank	Pitcher	Season	Consecutive QS
1	Jacob deGrom	2018	24
2	Bob Gibson	1968	22
-	Chris Carpenter	2005	22
4	Johan Santana	2004	21
5	Luis Tiant	1968	20
-	Mike Scott	1986	20
-	Jake Arrieta	2015	20
8	Robin Roberts	1952	19
-	Tom Seaver	1973	19
-	Jack Morris	1983	19
-	Greg Maddux	1998	19
-	Josh Johnson	2010	19
-	Jon Lester	2014	19

While there have been longer streaks spread over multiple seasons, no pitcher since World War II threw more consecutive quality starts in one year than Jacob deGrom this year. The fact that he did in a year in which quality starts were the rarest they've ever been adds to the accomplishment.

—*Rob Mains is an author of Baseball Prospectus.*

Heads-Up Hacking—The First Pitch

Matthew Trueblood

Batters fell behind in a higher percentage of all plate appearances in 2018 than in any previous season for which we have pitch-by-pitch data. That kind of granular information goes back only to 1988, but we might safely assume (given all we know about baseball as it had been before that, and as it has been in the years since) that batters have *never* fallen behind at a higher rate than they did last season.

Through the 1990s, the percentage of all plate appearances that began 0-1 hovered in the high 30s and low 40s. In the 2000s, it rose steadily but slowly, through the mid-40s. In 2018, 49.8 percent of all trips to the plate began 0-1. That, as much as anything, captures in microcosm the nature of hitting in MLB today.

A countdown clock toward strike three begins ticking almost the moment a batter takes his place in the box. The league's adjusted OPS+ on the first pitch was higher in 2018 than ever before, and that has been true in most of the last 10 seasons. Batters hit .264/.289/.442 in all plate appearances in which they swung at the first pitch last season, and .241/.330/.395 in all plate appearances in which they took that first offering.

The percentage differences in batting average and isolated power there favor swinging at the first pitch by more than in any season since 1988, while the difference in on-base percentage favors taking by more than ever. If you want to get on base at a decent clip, it's a good idea to be patient, but you run the risk of missing the only chances you'll get to produce power.

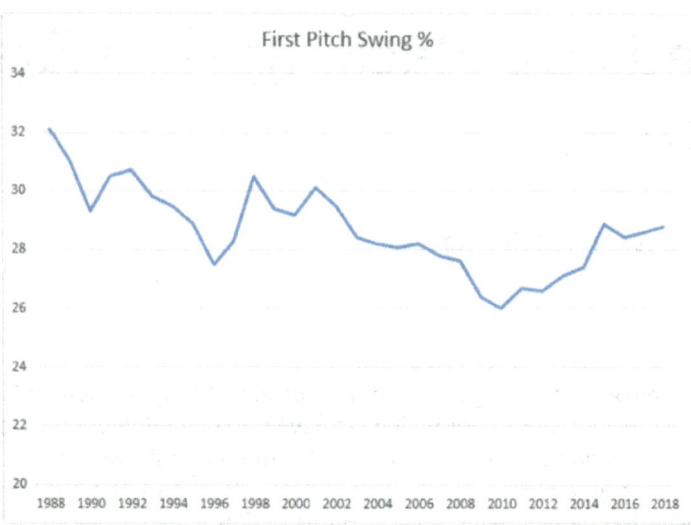

The league swung at the first pitch 28.8 percent of the time in 2018. With the isolated exception of 2015, that's the highest that number has climbed since 2002, but it might not be high enough. With the help of BP research maven Rob McQuown, I looked at the aggregate Called Strike Probability (CSProb) on the first pitch for each season since 2008, when the implementation of PITCHf/x first made measuring that possible. It's risen sharply during that period.

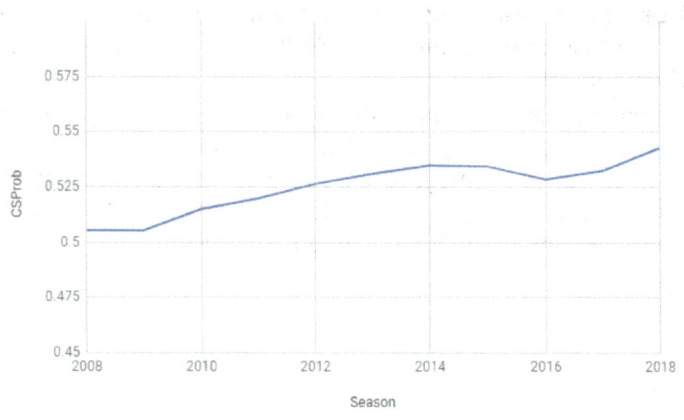

Called Strike Probability, First Pitch of PA (2008-2018)

Called Strike Probability is exactly what it sounds like: a pitch with a given CSProb has roughly that chance of being called a strike, if not swung at. In 2018, a batter who took 100 first pitches from a random sampling of the league's pitchers might expect to fall behind 54 or 55 times—up from 50 or 51 times in 2008. Almost regardless of pitch type (and, notably, especially in the case of fastballs), the first pitch tends to have more of the zone right now than ever before.

Pitchers are better at throwing strikes. They have better stuff, and believe more in their ability to miss bats within the zone. Perhaps most importantly, they know that batters are looking for one thing on the first pitch: a fastball. If they don't get it, they're likely to take the pitch. Check out how the use of sinkers and four-seamers on the first pitch has changed in a decade:

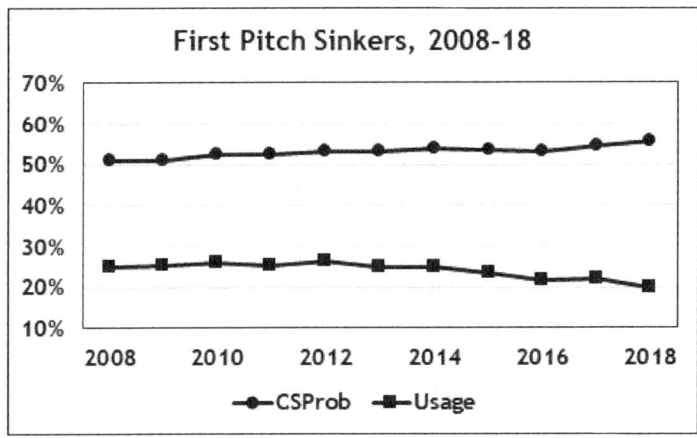

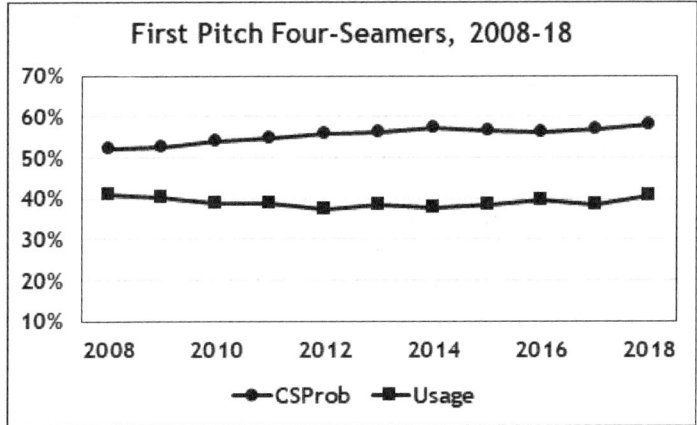

The sinker is losing its place in baseball, but the rate at which pitchers have thrown it on the first pitch hasn't dropped any faster than its usage rate in other counts. Pitchers have actually gone to their four-seamer *more* often to open counts, in the last few years, after a dip in the 2012-2015 period. What's really changed, though, and what shows up in both charts above, is that pitchers are catching more of the zone with first-pitch fastballs than they were a decade ago, or a half-decade ago. They're attacking right away, even with the pitch they know batters are expecting. The message is pretty clear: batters are being too passive.

Sliders, curves, and changeups each have more of the zone when thrown on the first pitch than they did several years ago, too, though the effect is less pronounced. Pitchers have seen the numbers; they know batters are doing better on the first pitch itself. They still feel safe throwing more and better strikes than ever before, figuring they'll come out ahead as long as they keep getting ahead to open each battle.

The Moneyball revolution brought an increased league-wide focus on OBP, which resulted in a de facto mandate to take a more patient tack at the plate. It worked very well for a while, as batters with poor plate discipline were compelled to either adjust or be expelled from the league, and pitchers with poor control were slowly weeded out.

However, concurrent with that revolution, and spurred by it in some ways, was the evolution of the pitching paradigm that now dominates the game. As batters ratcheted up their focus on inflating pitch counts and working walks, pitchers honed theirs on throwing strikes and missing bats. The league's understanding of what makes a good pitcher improved at least as much, from the mid-1990s through the mid-2000s, as its understanding of what makes a good hitter. As amphetamines and other performance-enhancing drugs were phased mostly out of the game, and as PITCHf/x broke onto the scene, individuals and teams learned how to exploit the evolved approaches of even the smartest hitters.

The ability to avoid making outs is still the most valuable one in baseball, but the magnitude of its eclipse of slugging is smaller than ever. To a greater extent than power, on-base skills derive their value from chaining—from the on-base skill levels of the players on either side of a given individual. Eleven years ago, when the housing crisis hit, people learned the hard way that the value of their homes depended a good deal on the values of their neighbors' homes. The same wasn't true, though, of their cars. So it is now, with OBP and SLG.

The global OBP in 2018 was .318. The only seasons since the Dead Ball Era in which the league got on base at a worse clip were 2013-2015, 1988, 1971-1972, and 1963-1968. This is all happening despite the aforementioned evolution of the science of hitting. It's happening despite a shift in approach and focus, one that would steer OBP ever higher, if only it were working.

Instead, it's sitting at a low ebb, and while it does so, even guys who get on base often are a little less helpful than they were 10 years ago—or 20, or 40, or 60, or 70, or 80, or 90. They're less helpful, that is, because unless there happen to be three or four other guys in the lineup who get on just as regularly, their contribution is merely to forestall the inevitable. Runs happen, increasingly, when a sudden bang happens, and that means attacking early in the count—because pitchers are sure as hell doing that.

In a league making contact on barely 75 percent of its swings, and a league in which an increasing number of pitchers can throw multiple off-speed pitches for strikes in any count, the only way to consistently generate offense is going to be aggressive. This isn't necessarily true for individuals, like Mookie Betts and Jose Ramirez, who make a lot of contact and have excellent plate discipline, and whose power comes from such natural quickness in a short stroke. Most players have to make tradeoffs, though, whether it be lowering their contact rate or raising their chase rate, in order to consistently make the quality of contact necessary to survive in today's game.

Highest %	Lowest %
Javier Baez – 48.3	Joe Mauer – 4.6
Freddie Freeman – 47.1	Mookie Betts – 9.7
Ozzie Albies – 46.3	Brett Gardner – 10.7
Jose Altuve – 44.2	Jose Ramirez – 12.0
Nick Castellanos – 44.1	Jason Kipnis – 13.8
Joey Gallo – 42.3	Jesus Aguilar – 14.5
Corey Dickerson – 40.9	Xander Bogaerts – 15.8
Salvador Perez – 40.8	Brian Dozier – 16.3
Eddie Rosario – 40.7	Mike Trout – 17.6
Nick Ahmed – 40.4	Yasmani Grandal – 17.6

Top 10 and Bottom 10 Hitters, First-Pitch Swing Rate (2018)

The question isn't which of these lists one prefers, but what they each convey, qualitatively, about the cat-and-mouse game of early-count hitting. Those top five on the left, especially, drive home the fact that for most players, getting aggressive early in the count is now key to keeping strikeout rate down and hitting for power.

For now, the message is: pitchers are coming right after batters with the nastiest stuff they've ever had. Batters had better stop giving away strike one and force hurlers to adjust, or the global OBP crisis is only going to get worse.

—*Matthew Trueblood is an author of Baseball Prospectus.*

A Hymn for the Index Stat

Patrick Dubuque

We survived without computers. I know this, because I remember the day when my dad hooked up his brand-new Atari 400 computer to the back of our 12-inch Magnavox television, and the perfect blue of the memo pad lit up for the first time. I was born just on the edge of that transitional generation, of learning cursive and balancing checkbooks and just doing math all the time, constant manual arithmetic.

It still amazes me. We learned how to sail ships without computers. We learned how to do calculus. We built towers that didn't fall down, most of the time. We engineered catapults to knock them down anyway. We built a robust system of philosophy called "utilitarianism," founded on the principle that the good of an action is evaluated by summing the effects of that action, which is the kind of formula that would make the world's mainframes crash. The whole foundation of statistics as a field is "here's math you could easily do but would die of old age first."

The fact of the matter is that there is too much math in the world to do. There are too many things changing, and too many things too small to notice, for us to handle. At some point, they become too much for the computers to handle as well, which is why we have chaos theory and undetectable earthquakes, but it's not an even fight. At some point, we fall back on intuition, and given how under-equipped we are, we're forced to bestow that intuition with some sort of supernatural superiority, the "gut feeling," that we can't prove because we can only intuit that our intuition is better.

We're all lousy at intuition, and wonderful at lying to ourselves about it. The honest truth is that computers are far better at intuition than we are, because in order to know what feels "off" you have to know what's "on." In order to do that you have to constantly reassess the average of everything, then re-rank your own experience against it.

Test your own, by comparing these three anonymous lines:

Player	G	HR	AVG	OBP	SLG
Player A	156	38	.259	.342	.535
Player B	154	38	.280	.348	.527
Player C	158	38	.266	.343	.509

These all seem like pretty similar players, right? The second one a touch more batted-ball dependent, the third a little less strong, but all pretty good hitters. And you'd be right, about the latter. Not the former.

Here's the breakdown:

- Player A: 1991 Howard Johnson, 141 DRC+
- Player B: 1996 Dean Palmer, 121 DRC+
- Player C: 2018 Giancarlo Stanton, 114 DRC+

Baseball is fortunate to have escaped the seismic shifts of so many other sports, where the talents and performances of other eras are nearly unrecognizable. (And not just other sports: try to explain the greatness of the movie Duck Soup without adjusting for era.) But they're still there, and they're nearly impossible to account for manually, without having to resort to sweeping generalizations like "steroid era" or juiced-ball era" to throw out entire swathes of production.

This is all to say that we should celebrate the index stat, that simple 100-based scale with such a humble aim: just to give context. It's hard to imagine how we lived without them for so long. Sabermetricians have always tried to make their stats look like other stats: True Average mapped to batting average, FIP molded to look like and compare to ERA. It's easy to understand the motivation—these statistics carry an emotional value in them that is hard to resist, as with the .300 hitter and the 2.00 ERA—but even they fall prey to the same loss of scale as their unadjusted counterparts. If a .300 average means different things in different years, does that hold true for a .300 True Average?

Instead, 100 doesn't say anything, except above average or below. And it does it instantly, for every season in every run environment for any statistic we want it to. We should have more index stats: K%+, so we can stop comparing Mike Clevinger's career 9.46 K/9 to Nolan Ryan's 9.55. HBP%+, so we can note that Ron Hunt was getting plunked when nobody else was getting plunked, as opposed to that imitator Brandon Guyer. Some might note how stale these references are and accuse league-adjustment as a backward-looking drive, and this is true. But we're always looking backward, always comparing the new with the expectations already set. The index stat just forces us to be honest.

There's always resistance to a new statistic, especially one so outwardly simple and so internally complex. We tend to stick with what we know, even in the case of formulas that are supposed to tell us what we know. But if your resistance is that it seems too complicated, too counterintuitive, too "black boxy," I encourage you to consider why you feel that way. Because the real world is infinitely more complicated than baseball, where all the pitches go in one basic direction and the baserunners are only allowed to travel in four directions. Baseball statistics based on mixed methodology are almost impossibly intricate. So are skyscrapers and automobiles. That's why we have computers—to take the guesswork out of them.

—*Patrick Dubuque is an author of Baseball Prospectus.*

Index of Names

Adam, Jason	51	Kennedy, Ian	71
Bailey, Homer	53	Kowar, Jackson	101, 105
Barlow, Scott	55	Lee, Khalil	87, 104
Blewett, Scott	93	Lively, Ben	101
Bonifacio, Jorge	20	Lopez, Jorge	73
Boxberger, Brad	57	Lopez, Nicky	88, 106
Bubic, Kris	94, 108	Lovelady, Richard	96, 111
Cancel, Gabriel	99	Lynch, Daniel	97, 107
Cuthbert, Cheslor	22	Machado, Andres	101
Del Rosario, Yefri	101, 110	Maldonado, Martin	34
Diekman, Jake	59	Matias, Seuly	89, 103
Dozier, Hunter	24	McCarthy, Kevin	75
Duenez, Samir	99	Melendez, MJ	90, 104
Duffy, Danny	61	Merrifield, Whit	36
Fillmyer, Heath	63	Mondesi, Adalberto	38
Flynn, Brian	65	Newberry, Jake	101
Gallagher, Cameron	26	O'Hearn, Ryan	41
Gigliotti, Michael	112	Oaks, Trevor	77
Goodwin, Brian	28	Owings, Chris	43
Gordon, Alex	30	Peralta, Wily	79
Gore, Terrance	85	Perez, Salvador	45
Greene, Conner	101	Perkins, Blake	99, 110
Griffin, Foster	101	Phillips, Brett	47
Gutierrez, Kelvin	99, 109	Pratto, Nick	91, 107
Hahn, Jesse	95	Rivera, Emmanuel	99
Hamilton, Billy	32	Schwindel, Frank	99
Hernandez, Carlos	101, 109	Singer, Brady	98, 105
Hill, Tim	101	Skoglund, Eric	81
Isbel, Kyle	86, 109	Soler, Jorge	49
Junis, Jake	67	Sparkman, Glenn	83
Keller, Brad	69	Starling, Bubba	99

Kansas City Royals 2019

Staumont, Josh 99, 111
Tillo, Daniel 111
Viloria, Meibrys 92, 111

Ballpark diagrams for Baseball Prospectus are created by THIRTY81Project, a design concept offering original ballpark artwork, including the new 'Ballparks of 2019' 11 x 17 color print.

Visit **www.thirty81project.com** for full details.